In Search of the Unchurched

Alan C. Klaas

An Alban Institute Publication

The Publication Program of The Alban Institute is assisted by a grant from Trinity Church, New York City.

Library of Congress Catalog Card Number 95-83893
ISBN 1-56699-169-2

CONTENTS

ACKNOWLEDGMENTS

Appreciation for assistance in preparing this book is expressed to the people at Aid Association for Lutherans who were instrumental in funding the project. President Dick Gunderson and the AAL board of directors provided ample funding and encouragement. Fraternal vice-president Glen Ocock allowed wide operational latitude for project activities. Without that freedom, the project would have not been sufficiently flexible to pursue new directions when unexpected opportunities arose. Fred Pahl and Doug Olson provided stability and assistance to a rapidly evolving line of study.

Cheryl Brown deserves special recognition for the substantial role she played in the project. Cheryl provided key insights at critical design and interpretation stages of several studies. She was instrumental in keeping everyone focused on the core issue—our Lord's Great Commission.

Twenty-three researchers from varied backgrounds and disciplines participated in data collection. The appendix lists the data collection leaders. These people are skilled researchers. They are also enthusiastic about the work of the church. Their determination to discover true solutions resulted in a successful effort.

Beth Ann Gaede was particularly helpful in the editing process. Her skill at editing and interest in the topic increased the clarity of the text.

The people at The Alban Institute deserve special thanks for their work in improving this book. Celia Allison Hahn's support and encouragement made this book possible. Her suggestions were always helpful. Her energy for the project is greatly appreciated.

Most of all, my wife, Joan, and our three children, Jennifer, Bethanie, and Melissa, deserve a special note of thanks. The project that led to this book required me to be away from home often. Even when I was home, the project demanded my time and drew my attention away from these important people. Thank you for your support and patience.

INTRODUCTION

Things were going so well. Congregations were springing up all over the place and growing rapidly. Denominations were dramatically increasing budgets and staffs and adding new ministries. Mission work was expanding. From the first days on Plymouth Rock through the twentieth century, it was hard for the church in the United States to keep up with itself.

In the 1970s, a few prophetic people started to talk about problems. In the midst of booming growth, their words received the treatment usually accorded prophets: they were ignored. In the 1980s most church people began to sense that something was wrong. Their usual solution was to work harder at what they were already doing. By the 1990s even the secular press was highlighting major problems in mainline denominations.

A remarkable number of trees have been sacrificed in the process of studying and writing about what has happened to mainline Protestant denominations. Well over 100 major books, studies, and works analyze this serious situation. And yet, the problems persist.

An ambitious course of action began in 1991. The elected leaders of the three largest Lutheran church bodies and the largest Lutheran fraternal benefit society decided to explore reasons for declining membership in Lutheran congregations. The three Lutheran church bodies were the Evangelical Lutheran Church in America (ELCA) and the Lutheran Church-Missouri Synod (LCMS). The Wisconsin Evangelical Lutheran Synod (WELS) was an active observer of the project. The fraternal society was Aid Association for Lutherans (AAL).

All four organizations agreed to

* conduct a major project that would set in motion forces to reverse the trend of declining membership.

*   ask an experienced researcher to lead the project. This person
        needed to be loyal to the mission of the church but not have ties to
        any particular church program, structure, or activity.

In Search of the Unchurched is the result of that two-year, million-
dollar project. This book has two primary messages. First, the most potent factor in declining membership is the change from a churched to an
unchurched society. Second, the best hope for dealing with the changed
society is the individual congregation.

The conversation then took an interesting twist. The group discussed
Several simple realities strongly impacted the project and this book.
These realities came to light during an everyday activity at the beginning
of the project. A group of project personnel stopped to refuel their rental
car. The youngest passenger remarked, "This is one of the better Quick
Stops in the area." A slightly older passenger observed, "I remember
when we called them gas stations." The oldest person in the group
countered, "I remember when we called them service stations." The
senior passenger went on to describe cheery attendants who checked the
oil, cleaned the windows, and checked air pressure in the tires, and did
not expect a tip for their service. Everyone in the car listened in silent
awe as the senior passenger described ancient history.

The conversation then took an interesting twist. The group discussed
the following six pairs of questions:

> What were gas stations like thirty years ago?
> *What are they like now?*
> What were grocery stores like thirty years ago?
> *What are they like now?*
> What were hardware stores like thirty years ago?
> *What are they like now?*
> What was transportation like thirty years ago?
> *What is it like now?*
> What was communication like thirty years ago?
> *What is it like now?*
> Where did people spend time thirty years ago?
> *Where do people spend it now?*

The passengers enjoyed describing personal experiences about the
"good ol' days." Then the discussion turned to another pair of questions:

Is the church affected by similar changes?
Is the church a place of refuge from uncomfortable change?

How you respond to these last two questions predicts your reaction to this book. Some people say the church must change. This book will stimulate change-oriented people. Other people say the church is a welcome refuge from the chaos of change. This book will be stimulating *and* a bit troubling for people who seek stability.

This book offers many comparisons that are helpful to those trying to understand what has happened to mainline denominations in the last twenty years. It is intended for people who are valiantly trying to distinguish what can be changed from what is unchangeable.

This book contains no predictions. It describes functional truths about the church thirty, forty, and fifty years ago, the church in which most churched people were trained and grew. These observations about the church of the past are contrasted with descriptions of new realities. There are no criticisms, only descriptions. The attempt here is to describe accurately and compare "what was" with "what is."

If possible, read this book with other key people in your ministry. Discussing the material with other ministry leaders will increase its value to you. More important, the payoff to your church's ministry will be enhanced when several people become enthused about the same issues.

This book describes many specific congregational activities. Some will apply in your ministry situation. Others will not. Discussing the ideas with a study group will generate even more ideas and create more possibilities, which can lead to more effective action. (There is an old saying about productivity: "One of the best ways to increase productivity is to do something.")

Chapter 1 presents seven paired concepts. Each pair articulates a key difference between the church twenty or thirty years ago and the church today. These seven pairs had a profound effect on the shape of the overall research project.

Chapters 2 through 9 describe the search for solutions to the problem of declining membership. Amazingly, millions of people are not aware there is a problem, although a large amount of information about the problem is already available. Chapter 2 concludes with a simple question: With so much excellent research and so many well-crafted explanations available, and with so many concerned Christians addressing this issue, why has so little progress been made?

Chapter 3 starts the analysis by concentrating on implications of the most effective source of solutions—individual congregations. To say this is a congregational issue may seem absurdly obvious. Yet the potential impact congregations can have on the declining membership problem seems to be relatively unexplored by denominational leaders.

Chapters 4 through 9 compare congregations that are achieving our Lord's Great Commission with those that are not. The key differentiating factors are described.

Chapter 10 follows the format of chapter 1 and presents fifteen specific ways changes in society as a whole have affected congregations and church bodies. The differences affect everyone who struggles to use trusted techniques developed for societies and church cultures that no longer exist in most places.

Chapter 11 concludes the book with a reminder about exactly why we are here. We are not building earthly kingdoms. We are winning souls for Jesus. Focusing on the goal of ministry is at the heart of finding solutions to declining membership and related problems.

CHAPTER 1

Things Were Going So Well!

How do you feel when you hear the word *change*? Some of us feel pleased and eager. Some of us feel angry and entrenched. Most of us are a bit leery.

Bill Bridge's masterful book on dealing with change, *Transitions: Making Sense of Life's Changes*, uses a different word—*transition*. For many of us, *change* means "revolution." *Transition*, on the other hand, tends to imply "evolution." *Change* usually implies stress, whereas *transition* sounds more natural. *Change* sounds abrupt, whereas *transition* feels smooth. *Transition* is a helpful, almost soothing term for an unsettling experience.

Most of us are so busy in our ministries that we do not notice the transitions. What we do notice is that many of the tried-and-true procedures no longer yield the desired results. When we look around for answers, we often find even the questions have changed. Some of us view this difference as "the threat of change." Others view this reality as "the challenge of transition."

For some of us, this chapter describes "change." For most of us, this chapter describes "transition." For all of us, this chapter articulates key functional differences between what used to be true and what is true now.

The seven transitions described in this chapter have an overarching impact on almost everything the church tries to do. These transitions have had a particularly dramatic impact on congregations, fundamentally altering what works and does not work in congregations, which should in turn have a dramatic effect on all organizations responsible for supporting the activities of congregations.

In one sense, these seven transitions have general societal implications. But try to resist the temptation to think about them as major or global societal issues. Rather, consider these transitions in the context of congregations. In fact, consider them in the context of *your* congregation.

Set aside, too, the natural tendency to consider these transitions in the context of what other people should be doing. While other people may need to take these matters into account, remember you can have the biggest impact on your own work. Concentrate on your specific church work.

This chapter is unusual in two fundamental ways. First, three kinds of type are used. As mentioned above, the chapter consists of seven paired concepts. The first half of each pair describes a characteristic of the churched society. Roman type is used.

The second half of each pair describes the corresponding current church reality, what is largely in place already. Some current realities are not yet fully functional. Others are well established and growing rapidly. Italic type is used in these sections.

A key question accompanies each pair of concepts. You are invited to write a response before proceeding. The question can also start study group discussion. Questions are in bold face type.

Second, you will need a pencil or pen and paper to read this chapter. You are asked to write in order to read. Use a writing tool, not a highlighting tool.

Transition 1: We have shifted from a churched society to an unchurched society.

Loren Mead's landmark book, *The Once and Future Church*, describes aspects of the "Christendom Era." From A.D. 315 until the 1970s or 1980s, the Christian church was heavily entwined with society as a whole.

Emperor Constantine proclaimed Christianity to be an acceptable religion of the empire. Purges, crucifixions, and one-sided bouts with lions came to an end. Overt persecution of Christians ended. The Middle Ages saw church and society more fully merged. The last few centuries have witnessed close relationships between the church and society.

In the United States, we put "In God We Trust" on our money. A public school day often started with a word of prayer. A community celebrated the Christmas season with a nativity scene in a public park.

With apologies to Mead, this book will substitute the term "churched society" when discussing the Christendom Era. The revised term is certainly not necessarily better, but it is clearer for the purposes of this book.

Mead's book goes on to describe the transition to the "Post-Christendom Era" in the 1970s or 1980s. The exact date of the transition is different in various parts of the country, within individual congregations, and in the minds of individual people. The exact transition date is not important, but the reality of transition is critical.

The relationship between church and society is not what it was twenty years ago. Teachers starting the public school day with a word of prayer lose their jobs. Communities cannot afford the legal fees they would have to pay to defend celebrating Christmas with a nativity scene in a public park. Everyone can cite a substantial list of ways Christianity has become separated from society. This book uses the term "unchurched society" when discussing current times.

What is the one most significant way your specific work with the church is affected by the transition from a churched society to an unchurched society?

_____

_____

_____

_____

_____

TRANSITION 2: **People participate in congregations for different reasons.**

In the churched society, people of faith automatically participated in a congregation. Attendance at weekly worship was a given. Sometimes people said, "Grandma would roll over in her grave if we were not in church." That phrase was particularly pertinent in many rural congregations because Grandma is buried twenty-five feet from the front door of the church sanctuary.

People of faith participated in a congregation no matter what was happening in the congregation. If the preaching was bad, they would still come. If the worship music was weak, they would still come. If the leaders were fighting, people would still come.

Not participating in a congregation was a sign of not having faith, and it was assumed that discussing religion with unchurched people meant bringing the good news of salvation to people without faith. People understood faith as the realm of the Holy Spirit, and congregations would simply preach the word. Doing more was a self-aggrandizing insult to the power of the Holy Spirit.

In the unchurched society, most unchurched people have separated the miracle of faith from the act of congregational participation. Virtually all research on attitudes of unchurched people has yielded the same findings. Between 70 percent and 85 percent of unchurched people identify religion as important or very important in their lives. Between 40 percent and 60 percent of unchurched people report praying to God daily or weekly. These people identify themselves as having faith but choose not to participate in a congregation.

The notion that people of faith would choose not to participate with their fellow believers seems unacceptable to a churched person still operating with the rules of the churched society. People living under churched society rules have a very difficult time understanding this transition. Church society Christians cannot imagine a person of faith choosing not to participate with the community of believers. Nevertheless, this apparent paradox is reality for over 70 million unchurched people living in the United States.

If the preaching is weak, people do not return to the congregation. If the congregation is only interested in itself, people do not join. If the congregation's leaders are fighting, people do not participate.

Some congregations have taken seriously the separation of the miracle of faith from the concept of congregational participation. These congregations are actively communicating the truths of their faith in ways that touch the hearts and souls of unchurched people. These congregations are removing barriers to congregational participation. Many of these congregations retain the time-tested activities preferred by long-term members who still function as if they were in a churched society. At the same time, these congregations find creative and unique ways to touch the lives of unchurched people.

People have separated the miracle of faith from the concept of congregational participation. What is the most powerful impact the separation has had on your current ministry activity?

_____

_____

_____

_____

_____

TRANSITION 3: **People have less loyalty to denominations.**

People were proud members of particular denominations. They knew the specific denomination in which their congregation held membership. They could name the leaders and officers of that denomination.

When people moved to a new community, they sought a congregation affiliated with the denomination of their ancestors. People purchased homes because of proximity to a church of the denomination they had always attended. People would drive many miles past two Lutheran Church in America congregations and one American Lutheran Church congregation to attend a Lutheran Church-Missouri Synod congregation. Neighbors would ask new residents, "What kind of church do you attend?" and then provide directions to a congregation affiliated with that denomination.

When people retired, they often moved to Sun Belt communities. Sometimes the new community did not have, for example, a Methodist congregation. Eventually enough Methodist's would gather in the new retirement community to start a "mission" congregation. The mission drew other Methodists new to the community. This pattern reflected most mainline denomination "mission planting."

In the unchurched society, some people still care about denominational affiliation and actively follow the workings and activities of their denomination. But, most members do not know or care about their congregation's denomination. Research with active lay leaders of congregations constantly shows lack of knowledge about the denomination. Many, perhaps most, congregation lay leaders express little interest in what the denomination is doing.

When the activities of a congregation no longer meet the needs of people in the unchurched society, they simply move on to another congregation. The denomination of the new congregation is not important. Often these people simply drop out of any congregation.

When people move to a different community, they are less likely to seek out any congregation at all, much less one from their ancestral heritage. Pastors in retirement communities report that migrating northerners are "retiring from work in the wars of the congregation."

The new reality is that people join congregations, not denominations.

What is the most powerful implication this loss of denominational loyalty has for your current ministry activity?

_____

_____

_____

_____

_____

Transition 4: **Congregations have different purposes.**

The fundamental purpose of congregations in the churched society was to help believers become better believers. Members were interested in unchurched people, but primarily within the context of activities designed for members. Congregations spent the majority of their time and resources nurturing the social and spiritual life of their current members.

Regional and national expressions of denominations delivered faith strengthening activities for existing congregation members. Denominations designed education programs for children, youth, and adults. The programs focused on the needs and desires of current members of congregations.

Everyone tied participation in a congregation to the presence or absence of faith. If Grace or William were not members of any congregation, it was assumed they lacked faith in Christ. Grace and William were welcome to visit a congregation. If they fit in with the members, they could join. The congregation was not responsible for finding ways to help them fit in. If Grace and William stayed away, it must be because they had rejected the work of the Holy Spirit.

Congregations functioning in the unchurched society continue to help believers become better believers. However, they use substantially different methods. These congregations have modified their definition of themselves and work hard to reach beyond their current members. While paying attention to members' faith development, these congregations actively seek ways to extend that love to others.

Congregations functioning in the unchurched society adopt different methods of communicating with unchurched people. For example, current members may use terms like narthex and sanctuary. Outsiders like William and Grace may not know those terms. Congregations reaching out to William and Grace are willing to use terms like hallway and worship center. The specific terms are different, but the meaning is the same.

Congregations that bring large numbers of people into membership are exposed to ridicule and abuse by people from other churches. These outreach-oriented congregations find enough joy in our Lord's Great Commission that they are able to continue their work, despite brutal comments from their critics.

Congregations that function well in the unchurched society see themselves as reaching out to broken and hurting people with the healing message. How they communicate with their members is substantially different from the way they communicate with unchurched people.

Is the focus of your ministry to current members or on reaching out with a healing Jesus to broken and hurting people, especially to non-members?

TRANSITION 5: The mission field has moved.

In the churched society, "mission" meant bringing Christ to heathen people in foreign countries. Mission fields were in Africa, New Guinea, China, and other far-off places.

Congregations, and regional and national offices of denominations, organized effective programs to conduct mission activities in these far-off places. Financial resources from individual members were funneled through denominational structures to overseas mission sites.

If mission happened in the local community, it was usually with the downtrodden of society. Missions were established for homeless people, hungry people, prisoners, unwed mothers, and other groups of people not part of the mainstream of society. When congregations became involved in mission work, that usually meant local mission societies sent food, clothing, or financial resources to distant mission fields.

Congregations functioning in the unchurched society see themselves as mission outposts in a mission field. These congregations perceive mission as starting at their property line. As people leave the church building, they see a sign above the door that says, "You are now entering the mission field."

Effective congregations in the unchurched society actively support national and international mission activities. Unlike congregations in the churched society, congregations in the unchurched society also target mission activity toward unchurched people in their surrounding community.

Approximately 50 percent of a community's people are effectively unchurched. The percentage might be a little higher in urban areas and a little lower in rural areas. This startling assertion may appear to be incorrect when congregations canvas all neighborhood households. Usually the resident will say, "I go to XYZ congregation." In the churched society, that phrase generally meant they participated in a congregation. But, in an unchurched society, stating "I go to XYZ congregation" usually means, "I go to XYZ congregation faithfully once every three years for a major festival." Or it means the neighbor has been there once or twice in the last ten years.

Congregations that function in the unchurched society adopt operational principles similar to those of missionaries who work in a different culture using a different language. These congregations find it necessary to change the way they speak to the people in their community. These congregations adopt different forms of music and worship so they can communicate with the people in their community. Just because their neighbors speak English does not mean the language used in traditional churches is understood by people with no background in church life.

List the two or three principal things you would do differently in your current ministry if that ministry were located in a foreign country.

_____

_____

_____

_____

_____

TRANSITION 6: Different people do the mission work.

In the churched society, professionals did the mission work. These professionals were paid, full-time staff or part-time, experienced volunteers. A specific group of people did the mission work on behalf of their congregation, their regional association, or their denomination.

Funds were collected locally. Money passed through the denominational structure to pay for mission activities. National denominations had mission staff. These mission staff professionals secured the services of full-time missionaries and commissioned them to work in foreign mission fields.

A denomination's regional offices operated mission activities within their geographic area. They hired chaplains for hospital and prison ministries. Social workers operated half-way houses, missions, and shelters of various types.

Even congregations segmented the mission work of the congregation. Most congregations had an evangelism committee which was responsible for doing the mission work of the congregation. Sometimes other members of the congregation would participate in a few activities of the evangelism committee, but generally speaking, the mission activities of the congregation were the responsibility of a small group of people who functioned in isolation from the rest of the congregation.

Congregations in the unchurched society function as if they are on a mission field and believe everyone is involved in the mission work of the congregation. All members have evangelism responsibilities. In fact, many (perhaps most) congregations with effective outreach activities do not have an evangelism committee. They consider it dangerous to make a small group of people responsible for what should be everyone's responsibility. If they have an evangelism committee, it is a "teaching" group, as well as a "doing" group.

These congregations actively support world missions. They are among the largest contributors to the world mission activities of their denomination and other organizations. These congregations also actively support regional mission activities organized by the denomination or other entities. These congregations are willing to support activities outside their formal church structures or within parachurch organizations.

The defining difference for these congregations is that everyone participates in the mission activity of the congregation.

How would your work in your current ministry be different if the people saw themselves as personally involved in the mission of spreading the Gospel?

_____

_____

_____

_____

_____

TRANSITION 7: Different denominational communication systems are developing.

Prior to the mid-1980s, communication was basically a paper bound process. Communications flowed through organized channels from one portion of a church structure to another. A missionary in New Guinea needed the formal church structure as a means of communicating ministry needs.

Communication with individual members of congregations passed through official church structures. Membership lists were maintained by the congregation, and using congregational mailing lists was a complex process involving metal plates imprinted with names and addresses. It was virtually impossible for anyone beyond the local level to communicate individually with mission donors. Rather, communication about mission was largely accomplished through magazines, newspapers, and other print media. Occasionally a missionary on six-month furlough visited a local congregation.

Congregational ministry resources (hymnals, Bible class materials, youth programs, and so forth) were delivered through denominational channels. Offering congregational resources outside official denominational channels was virtually impossible. Congregation leaders looked only to the denomination for resources.

In the current society, methods of communication are dramatically different. Even the most remote foreign mission sites can maintain electronic records of contributions. Facsimile, telephone, and electronic mail capabilities provide a person in the jungles of Panama the opportunity to communicate directly with potential donors anywhere in the world. Video technology makes it possible for potential donors to "visit" the missionary. Communicating the power of a ministry no longer requires someone from the formal church structure to carry the message to those who might support that ministry.

People who provide services to congregations no longer need denominational communication systems to make their services available. Advances in computer storage technology and data base management programs now allow almost anyone to maintain accurate and accessible records about people who might utilize their services.

Since the mid-1980s, denominational communication systems are no longer necessary to link local missions with supporting congregations or members. Denominational systems can still be useful, but they are not required.

What has changed about the way people communicate with you now, compared with methods of getting your attention twenty to forty years ago?

_____

_____

_____

_____

CHAPTER 2

The Problem

The transitions described in chapter 1 have occurred over many years and at different rates in different parts of the United States. Consequently, they have not been widely acknowledged, even when they have finally been recognized. The transitions, however, have created big problems for organized religion.

Starting with the 1979 landmark book by Hoge and Roozen, *Understanding Church Growth and Decline*,[1] religious researchers have observed the early stages of decline in churches and have probed the reasons for that decline. Some people in organized religion were already acutely aware of the problem. Most were only generally aware of the downward trends.

Scores of studies have uncovered many interesting factors contributing to the decline of churches. Whole books detail important aspects of this problem. Hundreds of books and articles describe the causes and impact of baby boomers dropping out of almost everything. Publications lament the departure of baby boomers, baby busters, and members of the "thirteenth generation" from the ranks of church membership. Researchers identify trends toward self-reliance and individualism as a cause of decreased commitment to institutions. Thoughtful people all over the country discuss the effect on organized religion of sociological phenomena such as the breakdown of family structures. Researchers have now probed the data more deeply. Their findings add texture to the complexity of the problem. Four examples will illustrate:

1. A research team studied 500 people confirmed in Presbyterian congregations twenty-five years prior to the study. Two key findings were shocking:

* Forty-eight percent were no longer members of any congregation.
* Only 29 percent were still members of a Presbyterian congregation.[2]

2. An unpublished research study examined conflicting information about the number of Lutherans in the United States. In 1990, national pollsters estimated about twelve million people were Lutheran. That same year, however, the total baptized membership of all Lutheran congregations was about eight million people. The church bodies within the Lutheran denomination were missing about four million of the Lutherans estimated by pollsters.

Both numbers proved to be correct. A sample of "pollster" Lutherans was asked, "Do you have contribution envelopes from a church?" Virtually all adult, baptized members of Lutheran congregations annually receive a box of envelopes to use when making weekly financial contributions. Approximately two-thirds of these pollster Lutherans reported having contribution envelopes. The apparent counting error lead to the realization that one-third of all Lutherans are not members of any Lutheran congregation.

3. A study of 4,371 lay people and 886 clergy in Lutheran congregations provided helpful insights into attitudes about outreach. Fifteen congregational activities were listed. Lay people and clergy picked the top six "purposes of a local congregation." Evangelism was *not* one of the top six selected by 99 percent of the laity and 94 percent of the clergy. A more general concept, "bringing in new members," did not appear among the top six purposes selected by 70 percent of laity and 58 percent of clergy.[3]

4. One mainline denomination had just over 200,000 "back door losses" annually over the last ten years, out of a membership of just over five million. Most other denominations are experiencing proportional losses. Many religious researchers estimate that seventy million effectively unchurched people in the United States still report religion as important or very important in their lives. They simply choose not to participate in a congregation. Some have suggested that the fastest growing "denomination" is the "church of the unchurched."

Almost all the largest denominations are working on the same problems. Protestant, Catholic, and Jewish denominational researchers gathered at Brandeis University in the fall of 1991 to discuss congregational membership. Researchers experienced a feeling of déjà vu as they listened to researchers from other traditions describe each major tradition's issues. Problems being analyzed in one denomination were virtually the same as those being experienced by everyone else. While researchers gathered substantial evidence and presented a large number of theories about trends in churches, denominational membership, worship participation, and receipts continued to decline. There is little evidence of denominational intervention before 1985.

As in most organizations, the importance of institution-wide problems in the church was not recognized until financial problems became significant. In the last half of the 1980s, declining contributions could no longer keep up with central denominational budget needs. In the ten years from 1985 through 1995, most mainline Protestant denominations experienced significant drops in income.

Despite ten to twenty years of formal study of the problems, most mainline denominations continue to experience membership losses and financial shortfalls. In 1993, The Center for Social and Religious Research at Hartford Seminary reported results of a membership study. Fourteen Protestant denominations showed virtually no change in membership from 1968 through 1992.[4] The best that can be said for the last twenty years of denominational interventions is that the rate of membership decline seems to have slowed. With so much excellent research, so many well-crafted explanations, and so many concerned Christians addressing this issue, why has so little progress been made?

The picture of what has happened is both clear and cloudy. We can clearly see that demographic, psychological, sociological, and other factors have dramatically affected denominations. But what churches can do about these issues is cloudy.

CHAPTER 3

The Source of Solutions: Congregations

The major changes in society at large have profoundly affected every part of the church from top to bottom. In fact, even the definition of which part of the church is "top" and which is "bottom" has been a matter of intense discussion.

Some denominations have tried to deal with the problems by directly addressing the changes in society. Organized religion has attempted to influence United States domestic policy, foreign policy, educational policy, social service systems, the content of entertainment, and so on. These mighty efforts led Peter Drucker to comment at the 1992 Leadership Network conference in Denver: "The mission became subordinated to social causes. Let me say, any organization that forgets its mission dies. They have subordinated their mission. The lesson is that we must not forget our mission."[1]

Drucker's insight suggests two harsh realities. First, organized religion has had little impact on larger societal problems affecting denominations. This assertion is not meant to denigrate the dedicated church people who have achieved impressive but isolated solutions to social problems; it simply acknowledges the overall reality.

Second, efforts to cure societal problems have deflected the church from its primary purpose. Reversing downward trends requires that denominations work where they can be most effective. Organized religion will never impact societal problems unless denominations include on their roles a large number of strong, healthy, and growing congregations.

Solutions to membership and mission problems in the church and in society require focusing on what the church should be able to do well, and developing internal capabilities that hold the most promise. That insight affected the direction of the Church Membership Initiative study, causing the project to focus on congregations.

Seven general conclusions were drawn from the extensive data.

1. This is a congregational issue.

People join congregations, not denominations. If congregations are not effective, denominations will eventually lose effectiveness. When the congregational infrastructure weakens, eventually the denominational capability weakens. Pronouncements from podiums have not solved problems. Most problems of organized religion would be solved if the over 250,000 congregations in the United States were to strengthen themselves, increasing the number of adults confirmed or baptized, worship attendance, and mission spending by as little as 20 percent.

Seeing the congregation as the key to reversing downward trends led to the second and third general conclusions.

2. Congregations that want to grow *might* grow.

Some congregations have an overt desire to reach more people. Having the desire is important, but it is not enough. Some congregations are located in communities with declining population. Some congregations have lost the critical mass necessary to get off life support. Some congregations use 1960s outreach methods that do not impact the faith life of new people.

Some people are surprised by the need to state this second conclusion. They say, "Tell me how much time and money you spent to discover 'Congregations that want to grow might grow.'" These people are stunned to see the third major conclusion.

3. Congregations that do not want to grow will not grow.

At first glance, the third general conclusion seems ludicrous. *Of course*, a congregation that does not want to grow will not grow. Keep in mind, however, that almost every congregation says it wants to grow. Ask any pastor or lay leader whether increasing the membership is important. The response is an almost unanimous desire to reach more people.

Unfortunately, most congregations behave in ways that prevent them from reaching more people. Sometimes members overtly offend non-members. More common are subtle behaviors, invisible to current members, that keep new people from participating in the congregation. The next chapter details these overt and subtle offensive behaviors.

The fourth general conclusion was reached by observing people talking with each other about outreach. Actually, the conclusion comes from watching church people talk *past* each other. When church people use the term *outreach*, some assume one meaning and others assume a completely different meaning. The fourth conclusion is:

4. There are two different kinds of outreach.

Many congregations engage in a wide variety of outreach activities. In fact, there are two kinds of outreach activity, and the first does not necessarily result in the second.

Many congregations engage in "presence outreach." Presence outreach means touching the daily lives of people in the name of the church. Through presence outreach, the congregation provides some form of social service to the community. Examples are food pantries, clothing drives, soup kitchens, shelters, and sometimes various kinds of schools or day-care facilities. These important activities are presence outreach when they do not directly impact the spiritual lives of the people touched by the ministry. Most presence outreach activities are third-party contacts. Congregations hire a professional or find a volunteer to make the actual contact. The members may have brief contact with the people they are helping. But the members do not develop personal relationships with the people being helped.

Presence outreach is contrasted with "Great Commission outreach." Great Commission outreach means touching the spiritual lives of people, thus preparing fertile ground for the Holy Spirit to establish and nurture faith in Christ as Savior and Lord. Great Commission outreach can start with the same activities as presence outreach. The difference lies in the fact that the ministry touches the spiritual lives of the people being helped. Most Great Commission outreach activities are first-person contacts.

Great Commission outreach requires that the congregation have a presence in its neighborhood, but presence outreach does not necessarily affect the beliefs of people.

At first glance, the fifth and sixth general conclusions may seem ridiculous.

5. Size is not the issue.

6. Growth is not the issue.

Size and growth are not the issues. Many small congregations conduct very effective ministries. Many large congregations are slowly dying. In either setting, growth might or might not happen. If growth occurs, it is a side effect of effective ministry, not the goal.

The senior pastors of large, growing congregations describe their congregations in terms of personal ministry. These congregations become large by focusing on people. By effectively addressing the lives of people, the congregations are impacting larger numbers of individuals. These congregations keep accurate track of size and growth, but they do not see size or growth as the objective.

The seventh general conclusion of the total study reveals how the details fit together.

7. The key is the attitude of congregational leaders and members.

When congregational leaders and members focus on themselves, the congregation has decided to die. The only question is, how long will they linger before they languish? This assertion will seem outrageous to many people in internally focused congregations. Some of these internally focused congregations are large and doing many good things. Unfortunately these offended people have not looked at their average weekly worship attendance numbers over the last ten or more years. The fact that the congregation is slowly shrinking is not immediately obvious, so members reject what their own congregation's statistics tell them about their own future.

When leaders and members pay substantial amounts of attention to reaching people who are not already members, the congregation moves beyond survival and begins to thrive.

Chapters 3 through 11 focus on congregations. Some people will be reading this book with a discussion group. Each of the remaining chapters ends with topics to inspire group discussion or to help individual readers digest the main points in the chapters.

For Reflection and Discussion

Spend about ten minutes thinking about or sharing your initial reactions to each of the general conclusions presented in chapter 3.

1. This is a congregational issue.
2. Congregations that want to grow *might grow*.
3. Congregations that do not want to grow will not grow.
4. There are two different kinds of outreach.
5. Size is not the issue.
6. Growth is not the issue.
7. The key is the attitude of congregational leaders and members.

CHAPTER 4

Ministry to Members Only

Congregational attitude is the critical difference.

At the heart of membership and attendance problems is the attitude of congregational leaders about the purpose of the congregation. Information about demographic trends, sociological issues, and general societal changes provides useful background, but the congregation cannot do much to impact these trends, issues, and attitudes. The parish can only control how it responds to these realities.

Attitude about the central purpose of ministry distinguishes congregations that grow from those that do not. About 80 percent of congregations focus on ministry to current members. Even though some have social service programs such as food pantries, used-clothing closets, or similar activities, their primary focus is meeting the needs of current members.

Meeting member needs seems an obvious role for the local parish to play. In one sense, that is why congregations were formed. The problem comes when meeting member needs becomes the dominant focus. These congregations express interest in reaching people. At the same time, they refuse to adopt attitudes and activities required to reach people in the unchurched society. Sometimes these congregations are surprised and offended by the notion that they are not interested in following our Lord's Great Commission. Perhaps a few illustrations will help make this clear.

Have you ever heard someone say, "Adding a second worship service will destroy our congregation." This statement means, "We are not a congregation unless we all worship together all the time." Assuming that 30 to 50 percent of members worship each week, a congregation that expects everyone to worship together has decided never to have more members than two or three times the seating capacity of its sanctuary. The congregation's responsibility for reaching new people stops when seating capacity in the sanctuary is reached.

Have you ever heard someone say, "Adding members will damage the personal relationship between pastor and member"? This is true. People who study interpersonal relationships explain that an individual cannot have deep, one-on-one relationships with more than about 100 people. The work of Arlin Rothauge confirms this limit for a "pastoral church."[1] By this criterion, however, the congregation's responsibility to reach unchurched people stops when it has 50 to 150 active members.

Have you ever heard someone say, "Anyone is welcome to join us"? Actually the complete statement is, "Anyone is welcome to join us, *as long as they do things the way we do them now*." These congregations are not willing to consider the preferences or feelings of anyone who is not already a member. They have decided they have no Great Commission responsibility for neighbors who use different styles of communication.

Some congregations have the attitude, "Our community is declining, so why expect growth from us." Frequently these congregations have a long history of ministering only to their own members. They watch members move away or die. Sometimes they see their community decline in population. Sometimes they see new, but different, people moving into the area. Because these members focus on ministry to their current members, they feel helpless to deal with community changes.

Sometimes congregational leaders object to the notion that they have a responsibility to reach other people. The leaders state, "We are interested in spiritual growth, not numerical growth." The tone of the statement suggests spiritual and numeric growth are mutually exclusive. Frequently these leaders also make the companion statement, "If a congregation is growing, it must be compromising its theology." These congregations use theological positions as a reason to avoid personal responsibility for our Lord's Great Commission.

Every congregation describes itself as a "friendly congregation." Because of this belief, the "mystery shopping visits" research technique was a helpful tool for studying how friendly these congregations really are. Researchers adopted the role of strangers new to the community and visited worship services. The "visitors" arrived five minutes before a service, attended the service, and milled around after the service for five minutes. Our visitors often observed that members are truly close to each other. The visitors also observed how *closed* the members are to strangers.

Perhaps one example of this phenomenon will be helpful. A retired pastor spent six weeks visiting congregations where he was a stranger. The visits resulted in a few smiles and little else. Eventually someone spoke to him. The person turned out to be another first-time visitor.[2]

Chapters 4 through 6 include a large number of detailed descriptions of congregational attitudes and activities. Congregations can learn by examining whether these attitudes and activities are exhibited in their own situation. Action suggestions are provided for evangelism committees, planning committees, and other leadership groups.

Action Suggestion

Sometimes people think these examples of closed congregations are just extreme or isolated cases. Test the finding yourself. Pick ten congregations where you are a stranger and visit them. Be friendly, but do not go out of your way to make contact. You will be shocked at how you are treated.

Entry points provide access to congregations.

Another method of understanding a congregation's definition of ministry is to examine its "entry points." Analyze the monthly calendar or weekly list of activities. Classify events into three groups. Group 1 are events and activities for *members*. These include clubs, organizations, teams, and study groups. Group 2 events support the congregation's *structure*. These include boards, committees, choirs, and service groups. Group 3 events are attended by large numbers of people who are *not already members*.

In most congregations, you will find that most activities fall into the first two groups. These congregations have busy members. They have involved members; much is happening for them. Very little is happening for people who are not already members.

Many of these congregations contend that they invite people who are not members. "If other people chose not to come, that is their decision. We are not responsible." These are congregations focused on their current members, and they have only one entry point, one way people who are not already members might come into contact with the congregation. That one entry point is the weekly worship experience—conducted using one style of communication. Members are satisfied that the weekly service fulfills their total responsibility to follow the Great Commission. These congregations sometimes have several presence-outreach activities. Unfortunately, such activities rarely achieve Great Commission outreach results.

Action Suggestion

Examine two or three of your congregation's monthly calendars. Label each listed activity as Group 1, 2 , or 3. Count the events in each group. Share what you find with key congregational leaders.

Congregations with declining membership have identifiable characteristics.

Most congregations that focus on needs of current members are experiencing stability or decline in mission, ministry, and membership. These congregations have several common characteristics.

1. Members have a "poor me" attitude about their congregation.

When members are asked to describe their congregation, they usually start by expressing appreciation for the ministry they receive. Then they begin to say things like, "We are *only* a small congregation," "We are a *struggling* congregation," or "We are working hard to *stay open*."

These wonderful people of God describe their congregation in diminutive terms. They use adjectives indicating modest levels of depression and despair. The self-esteem of the members and their clergy is low.

A content analysis of their key leadership meetings yields interesting observations. The church council, vestry, session, consistory, or board meetings start with discussion of financial problems. The meetings then focus on all the problems, difficulties, complaints, and weaknesses.

If the agenda does not dwell on problems, it usually consists of many reports on unrelated activities. Much of the discussion focuses on internally directed work. Seldom is there cooperation between the various reporting boards and committees on a common issue. The entire group rarely focuses on working together to achieve a common ministry goal.

Analysis of planning retreats yields similar results. The leaders fill sheet after sheet of flip-chart paper with detailed lists of all the problems. The meeting room walls are lined with reminders of how poorly things are going. The meeting procedures force the group into the twin terrors of depression and despair. Frequently the leaders then decide to identify and tackle the two or three most difficult problems. That effort usually fails to yield desired results.

Action Suggestion

First, analyze the content of your parish leadership meetings. Differentiate between negative and positive topics. Second, assign the negatives to a few trusted people to resolve. Third, have everyone focus on one or two shared ministry goals.

Action Suggestion

First, analyze your major planning meetings. Second, add up how much of the time is spent listing problems. Third, stop listing problems.

2. Members are not aware of their congregation's strengths.

Most congregations experiencing stability or decline are simply not aware of their strengths. Why should they be? They spend so much time dealing with problems that they cannot see anything else.

Every congregation has strengths. Every congregation does something well. Every congregation has the ability to share a strength with others. Members can learn to identify their congregation's strengths. They have simply gotten out of the habit.

Action Suggestion

Kennon Callahan says it best. *Do not* begin by addressing your biggest problems. Start by identifying and expanding on a strength. Build positive experiences. Create some wins before tackling a modest weakness.[3]

---

3. Members are not involved in their congregation's neighborhood.

Virtually all congregations that focus on current members are *not* involved in the local neighborhood. The members are generally aware of what is happening in the neighborhood. In fact, they spend much time before and after meetings decrying what is happening in the neighborhood. Yet, their internal focus keeps the congregation from responding to their context.

Some congregations have become "island congregations." The members lived near the congregation for many years. The young people moved away. Many members relocated and transferred out of the congregation. Some members have moved out of the congregation's neighborhood but loyally drive back for worship and meetings. A few members still live in the neighborhood, but many of them yearn to leave.

The members come to the buildings on Sunday morning for worship. The members come on one or two evenings for meetings or choir rehearsal. Members who still live in the neighborhood often have no interest in or involvement with the neighborhood surrounding their island

congregation. In many locations, members view the neighborhood surrounding the congregation with a sense of apprehension or even fear.

Members hope their congregation will again be strong, that is, that it
will return to "the good old days." They comment about the need to "get
back to the way things were." At the same time, these members seem to
know that will never happen. They seem resigned to continued decline
until the last few members turn out the lights for the last time.

4. The congregation is served by a few, long-term lay leaders.

Most congregations focused on their current members describe leadership problems. The same people have been doing all the work for many
years. These people are tired, even burned out. The leaders are dismayed
that new leaders are not coming forward. Current leaders are particularly
troubled when their few young members do not accept leadership roles.

In most cases, the leaders themselves create the problem. Typically
the flow of events goes like this:

A new member is asked, or volunteers, to help.
The new person offers a new idea.
The new idea is greeted by one or more of the following comments:

*   "That is not the way we do things here."

*   "We have never done it that way before."

*   "We tried that once several years ago. It didn't work."

The message given to the potential new leader is, "We will not consider your idea." The more important lesson taught to the discouraged,
potential new leader is, "Do not come up with anything new."

In these congregations, the leadership problem is not a lack of potential new people to do the work. The problem is the work to be done.
Frequently, current leaders want new leaders, but only to conduct the
current, time-honored, time-tested activities.

Congregations focused on the preferences of their current members
are particularly vulnerable to this problem. Current members only know

what they are currently doing. If the current activities are not of interest to their few new members, the pool of workers available for current activities decreases. The current leaders themselves are the primary cause of the congregation's lack of future leaders

---

Action Suggestion

Look at the full list of congregational activities for last year. Mark the activities that were new last year. If the number is small (or zero), you are looking at an important reason you have trouble getting new leaders.

---

5. The congregation's community is declining.

Congregation leaders in rural and urban areas say, "Our community is declining, so why expect anything different from our congregation?" In rural areas the population may be decreasing and the young people may have moved away. A small community is seriously hurt when the county's consolidated school district closes the local elementary school or the farm implement store closes.

Rural communities are experiencing a host of economic and social problems.

The same general list of factors affects central city areas. The only difference is that in urban areas, there are still thousands of people in the neighborhood. The challenge is that there are fewer "people like us" in the neighborhood. The congregation is structured to meet the needs of "people like us." Usually the majority of the new people have different preferences for activities, music, worship style, leadership, and other important aspects of congregational life. The congregation has no means of connecting with its new, but different, neighbors. It becomes an island congregation.

Two factors are particularly striking about the reaction of congregations in what they see as declining neighborhoods. First, the congregational leaders feel helpless to reverse the congregation's experience. They try everything and "everything" fails. People insist, "What we are doing worked twenty years ago," but they do not notice the strategy is no longer effective. The congregation becomes a place of refuge, not a mission outpost. It insulates itself from the changes going on all around.

Second, there is usually a booming congregation in the neighborhood. In rural areas, the rapidly expanding parish might be some distance away. In urban areas, the growing ministry is usually just down the street. Most leaders of troubled rural and urban congregations are vaguely aware of their booming neighbor. Because shrinking congregations focus on their troubles, it never occurs to them that a simple visit to the booming congregation might be helpful.

Action Suggestion

If you are in a struggling congregation, visit a nearby booming congregation. The number of good ideas you will observe is amazing. Most of these ideas will not compromise your theology.

---

6. The congregation sets up invisible barriers.

Congregations focused on current members set up invisible barriers. These characteristics are *barriers* to outsiders but *invisible* to current members.

The best description of invisible barriers is from a network news interview of a person who calls himself "the Church Man." This individual visits churches on Sunday. He critiques the experience on a Monday radio program and evaluates the experience, awarding a rating of one to four bells.

The network reporter asked the Church Man to describe the congregation he had just visited. The Church Man replied:

"I went to the front door, but it was locked. There was no sign." (*Everyone* knows the parking lot is in the back, so there is no reason to unlock the front doors.)

"There were five entry doors from the parking lot behind the building. None of them were marked." (*Everyone* knows which doors to enter, so there is no need to mark them.)

"I picked a door and found myself in an office complex. I had to wander through the building to find the sanctuary." (*Everyone* knows how to find the sanctuary, so there is no need to put up direction signs.)

"I wanted to use the restrooms, but could not see where they were located." (Signs are not needed because *everyone* knows the restrooms are in the basement.)

These are all examples of barriers for unchurched visitors. Un-churched visitors are reluctant to be identified as visitors. They are shy about asking questions that reveal their ignorance. They do not know the unwritten rules and clues about directions or whom to ask for help. For-merly churched people are reminded of the kind of uncaring attitudes that drove them out of a congregation many years ago. Unchurched people are made to feel like unwelcome outsiders.

Members are generally appalled to learn about such experiences. Members perceive themselves as friendly, even though they generally ignore visitors. They do not know how lost and puzzled visitors feel because they themselves already know the answers. They cannot see the many problems they are creating.

A second example of invisible barriers comes from observing visi-tors in worship. A dying congregation in an ethnically changed neighbor-hood displayed this barrier. A few senior citizens regularly attended Sunday worship in this island congregation. The visitor was a fifteen-year-old young man from a heritage different from the congregation. He was visiting *by himself.* (Think about that for a moment: a fifteen-year-old—visiting a congregation of senior citizens from a different ethnic heritage—by himself.)

The young man received the worship guide, a sheet with Bible read-ings and prayers, the weekly announcements, a flyer about families, and the Sausage Dinner sign-up sheet. The hymnal was in the pew rack.

Five minutes into the service the congregation skipped a section of the hymnal's printed liturgy. The young man was immediately lost. A woman politely and quietly slid over to the young man. She pointed out the spot in the liturgy to which the congregation had skipped. (Think about how this young man feels: he was lost and now he is *publicly* lost.) Three minutes later, another unannounced skip occurred. The young man was lost again. What was he getting out of the service? Not much!

Adult visitors who experience this same treatment do not keep trying. They simply close the book and sit quietly until the service ends —or until they can duck out unobtrusively. Nine months of effort by an evangelism group in an each-one-reach-one program is wiped out five minutes into the service. After the service, these visitors will say to the pastor, "Nice service," as they proceed out the door and down the road, never to return.

These are invisible barriers, invisible to the congregation's members. The members know how to use the worship guides, which parts of the printed liturgy are skipped, when to stand, and when to sit. The members of congregations focused on their current members simply do not see these barriers.

Action Suggestion

Find two or three unchurched people. Ask them to visit your congregation. Ask them to make notes of everything that positively and negatively affects them—no matter how small. Ask these people to honestly and frankly report what they observe, how they were treated, and how they felt. You will find their comments helpful—and probably disturbing.

Do not use churched people for these visits. *Do not* exchange these visits with another congregation. Churched people will not be able to see the invisible barriers.

---

7. Members see themselves as a family.

Perhaps the most powerful characteristic of congregations with declining membership is that they see themselves as a family. In fact, they are a family. Ask yourself, How do people get to be members of a family? They are born into a family. They marry into a family. Only rarely are people adopted into families.

There are many positive aspects of family life that helpfully describe congregations. The warmth and acceptance of healthy families are desirable qualities for congregations.

Families (and congregations), however, are also closed systems.

They are very difficult to enter. When families (and congregations) have few young members, marriages and births can no longer replace deaths and departures. Without an external source of new members, families (and congregations) eventually disappear.

Action Suggestion

List the helpful aspects of "family" experienced in your congregation. List the unhealthy aspects of "family" experienced in your congregation. Discuss these two lists with your congregation's leaders.

For Reflection and Discussion

Discuss or think about your congregation's situation relative to the main points in this chapter:

1. Is our congregation focused on current members?
2. How many entry points do we *really* have? How effective are they?
3. Do we exhibit any of the characteristics of stable or declining congregations?

* Members have a "poor me" attitude about the congregation.

* Members are not aware of their congregation's strengths.

* Members are not involved in their congregation's neighborhood.

* The congregation is served by a few, long-term lay leaders.

* The congregation's community is declining.

* The congregation sets up invisible barriers.

* Members see themselves as a family.

Reflect on or discuss with your study group the potential value of each of the nine action suggestions contained in this chapter.

CHAPTER 5

Ministry beyond Members

About 20 percent of congregations have as their primary mission ministry beyond their current membership. These congregations continue to meet the needs of current members. However, they serve current members in different and exciting ways. These congregations diligently and effectively respond to our Lord's Great Commission in the neighborhood God has given them.

Action Attitudes and Activities

Each congregation that focuses on Great Commission outreach is unique. Few of these congregations use exactly the same programs and activities adopted by others. They define their congregation's response to the unchurched society by customizing their activities to their community. They have abandoned the churched-society notion that most congregations are similar to each other.

Congregations focused beyond their current membership have a few common characteristics. Interestingly, these unifying characteristics cause the congregations to be unique.

1. Outreach-oriented congregations are motivated to extend mission beyond current membership.

The strongest common characteristic of these congregations is their determination to extend the saving Gospel message to people who are not already in their congregation. These congregations recognize there are no "magic pills." No program, activity, or method will effectively reach others unless the congregation is *first* deeply committed to Great Commission outreach.

Many congregations adopt the "magic pill" approach to outreach. They say, "All we need to do is introduce new music." Others say, "All we need to do is get each member to invite someone else." Without making a total attitudinal and programmatic commitment to Great Commission outreach, most congregations bump from one fad to the next without achieving desired results.

Congregations committed to reaching the unchurched in their community and around the world do not rely on gimmicks and marketing techniques. They know that if these approaches result in large numbers of people coming in the front door, there usually are an equally large number of people going out the back door. *Congregations committed to reaching others for Christ understand that Great Commission outreach involves the total life of the congregation.*

Action Suggestion

Review your congregation's last outreach effort. Review the actual impact of that effort. If the impact was less than was hoped, list the other congregational characteristics you modified *before* the outreach effort started. Most outreach efforts come up short because they are "magic pills" rather than efforts integrated with other aspects of the congregation's total Great Commission outreach.

---

2. Outreach-oriented congregations seek local, contextual answers.

Congregations focused on ministry beyond current membership understand their neighborhoods. They develop activities that meet the needs of their neighbors. They are constantly alert for ideas that have proved helpful to other Great Commission outreach congregations. They recognize the need to adapt programs from other communities to the local situation. They recognize that the churched-society approach of using denominationally developed programs "out of the box" is no longer effective.

Perhaps two examples will be helpful. The ideas might surprise you, but both clearly illustrate the point that congregations need to deal with the congregation's context or neighborhood.

A pastor observed an increase in the number of hours spent counseling couples in the congregation with troubled marriages. The pastor concluded that married couples were losing touch with each other because the demands of their respective daily lives were leaving them with less in common.

The pastor of this rural, midwestern town decided to start a country western line dancing class. He said, "I know this class is not described anywhere in the Bible. What I wanted was an activity these couples could learn together. I wanted to do something fun that they could develop as a common interest."

This pastor developed a local, contextual response to a significant ministry issue. Helping marriages succeed is an important activity of the church. Operating this unusual class, within a Christian context, provided opportunity for couples to repair damaged relationships. The class is a living (and lively) extension of Christ's love.

Many people react negatively to this second example of an unusual Christian response to an important community issue. The congregation's reasons for adopting the unusual program, however, are persuasive.

Housing in the congregation's community consists predominately of starter homes for families with young children. The congregation initiated a program called "Potty Training with Jesus."

The pastor admits that most people are surprised to hear about this program, and some people are offended by the program's title. The pastor also acknowledged, "Using the Proverbs 22:6 suggestion to 'Train up a child in the way he should go' as a biblical basis for this program was a bit far fetched. But," he explained, "we simply felt there is no better time to teach the principles of Christian discipline than this first opportunity for a child to have a serious difference of opinion with his or her parents."

This congregation is known on the community grapevine as a place to come for help with this difficult parenting issue. The members are communicating important Christian principles in a manner appropriate to their neighborhood.

Both of these congregations are growing. They are not growing because of country western line dancing or potty training. They are growing because the congregations are committed to communicating the Christian message in a way that affects people who are not already members—as well as those who are members.

A list of all the specific examples we have encountered of parishes that respond to community needs with local, contextual answers would be very long. Studies of congregations that meet community needs describe groups for people recovering from various addictions, groups for victims or perpetrators of abuse, job seeker support groups, classes on managing family finances, and a host of other contacts with the community.

There is one important caution. Congregations interested in reaching unchurched people are *actively involved* in these programs and groups. They do not simply rent or donate space for an outside organization to use the facility. Renting a building is a form of presence outreach. Building rental is not Great Commission outreach.

Action Suggestion

Find or make a list of last year's outreach activities. Mark the activities in which members had more than a few direct contacts with nonmembers and for more than a few minutes. Compare the number of first-person community contacts with the total number of outreach activities. Pick any two of the outreach activities not marked. Decide how to make them first-person contacts with the community.

---

3. Outreach-oriented congregations meet people's needs, not needs of the organizational structure.

Congregations intent on reaching people who are not already members see congregational activities from a new perspective. They focus on ministry, not on the organization and structure of the congregation. When rules and procedures get in the way of ministry, the congregation changes the rules and procedures. If historical methods of operating are not supported, the methods are abandoned. Perhaps a few examples will illustrate the difference between structural approaches and ministry approaches.

A pastor explained that neighborhood families with young children preferred to leave their babies and toddlers in a nursery while the parents attended worship services. However, these people would only attend worship if the nursery was staffed by mature, adult women. That reality presented a problem: Mature, adult women were not willing to *staff the nursery*.

Most parishes simply give up on these outsiders who made unrealistic or improper demands. Not this congregation. From the perspective of this congregation, which was motivated to extend ministry beyond current members, analysis of the problem resulted in a new ministry focus. They understand that one reality of the unchurched society is that people, even active members, have low levels of interest in giving valuable time to structural issues.

Based on this understanding, the congregational leaders changed their perception of the nursery problem. They realized that *staffing the nursery* is a structural issue. The congregational leaders came to see their nursery situation as a mission issue. Mature, adult women were asked to support *a ministry that helps mothers of young children attend worship*. The ministry flourished. The problem was solved. The change from a structural approach to a missional approach was the key. The problem (staffing the nursery) was solved by creating a ministry (helping young mothers attend worship).

In another example, a consultant was visiting a struggling congregation. The consultant suggested that an open hour be used for visiting people. The pastor replied, "The closest member lives thirty minutes away. There is not enough time." The consultant said, "I was thinking about the house across the street where the moving van was yesterday."

The pastor and consultant crossed the street, ascended the stairs, crossed the porch, and knocked on the door. A woman opened the entry door but kept the screen door closed. The three-year-old daughter was standing behind her mother and clinging to her mother's leg, sneaking peeks at the callers.

The pastor introduced himself as being from the church across the street, welcomed the woman to the community, and asked about the distance and difficulty of moving. The pastor then described several parish activities of potential interest to this young mother. The pleasant conversation concluded with an invitation to attend worship the next Sunday.

Meanwhile, the consultant crouched down to eye level with the little girl. The consultant started the conversation by observing, "You look sad." The little girl replied, "I am sad." The exchange continued:

"Why are you sad?"

"I'm lonely."

"Why are you lonely?"

"I don't know anyone here. I miss my friends."

The consultant and little girl spent a few minutes talking about feeling sad and lonely. Then the consultant said, "Later this afternoon a group of girls your age will be at the church across the street. Would you and your mother like to come and meet some of them?"

Do you see the difference between these two types of evangelism calls? The pastor conducted a structure-based discussion. The consultant pursued a mission-based discussion. The pastor raised conventional topics. The consultant's conversation was centered on the driving force in the little girl's life. The success of the pastor's call rested on the churched-society perspective that people new to the community will seek out a congregation. The success of the consultant's call rested on the un-churched-society perspective that people respond to support for their hurts and hopes. In the unchurched society, the pastor's traditional invitation would be accepted once in a while. The consultant's ministry approach would be accepted most of the time.

4. Outreach-focused congregations organize around mission, not structure.

Congregations intent on reaching unchurched people remove structural barriers to ministry. Here again, a few examples best explain the difference.

A gentleman had been through a rough time with his teenage children. He found help and healing in the Scriptures and worked through the problems. He told the congregational leaders he was interested in sharing this knowledge and experience with others. The leaders referred him to the youth ministry committee.

After three months of deliberation, the youth ministry committee approved his proposal. The volunteer was then referred to the elders. Bible study was part of the program and the elders needed to be sure Scripture was going to be used appropriately. After another three months, the elders approved and referred the matter to the board of property management because the program required access to the building. Three months later the property people approved the plan and sent the matter to the church council. One church council member objected to a detail. The matter was returned to the youth ministry committee.

The ministry never happened. More important, this interested volunteer was taught, "Never come up with another new idea." The congregation was organized around structural controls. The structure assured that nothing happened unless everyone agreed beforehand. The congregation is dying.

A similar situation was handled very differently in a parish focused beyond current members. A woman had endured a particularly difficult divorce. She found help and healing in the Scriptures and was willing to share what she had learned.

The leaders referred her to the New Ministry Action Team. The team asked if she could start in two or three weeks and asked how she planned to promote the program. She explained her thoughts about placing an advertisement on the religion page in the local newspaper. The team offered to pay for the ad but thought the ad should not be on the religion page. The action team explained, "Only churched people read the religion page. Our congregation is looking for ways to contact people who are not already members of a congregation. Let's put your ad in the personals section."

A divorce recovery group started the next month. One year later the congregation was ministering to over 100 people recovering from divorce, a significant issue in the community. This congregation was organized to act on ministry opportunities.

Two more examples are from small, rural, midwestern towns dominated by agribusiness. Small, rural towns can endure great economic hardship and still exist as a community. However, when "the place for coffee" closes, the town is finished. The place for coffee is the nerve center of these towns. All community business is conducted over morning coffee at the luncheonette restaurant, barber shop, farm implement store, fire station, or wherever the town leaders gather before the work day starts. Official meetings of the bank board of directors or local government merely rubber stamp what is decided over morning coffee.

The place of coffee closed one week before a consultant arrived in the town to study a congregation. The people were grieving this devastating loss. The consultant suggested the congregation offer space for a replacement. The responses were, "Who will pay for the coffee? What about the supplies? Who will clean up? What about the insurance?"

Another congregation saw their town's place for coffee close two weeks prior to the consultant's visit. The same suggestion was made. The leaders responded with an enthusiastic, "Yes! Thank you for that helpful suggestion. We can probably get started next week. Let's get the word out right away."

The first congregation was organized around structural limitations. A wonderful ministry opportunity was lost. The second congregation was organized around mission. They became known in the community as a place of hope and concern. The second congregation did not let operational problems interfere with a ministry opportunity.

Action Suggestion

Name any boards, committees, or activities for which recruiting workers is hard. Discuss the possibility of approaching that need differently or simply not having the board, committee, or activity. Pick two of these difficult-to-fill groups. Drop one group for a year and see if it is missed. Decide to handle the other group's responsibilities in a different way for a year to see how that works.

---

5. Outreach-focused congregations use members' gifts in new ministries.

Congregations that actively reach unchurched people make extensive use of the ministry gifts of their members. Some denominational traditions call this practice the "priesthood of all believers." These congregations meet the ministry needs of their current members by channeling members' energies into Great Commission outreach activities. They do not sap the energy of current members with endless attention to structural matters.

Leaders of congregations that would like to reach beyond current members often are overwhelmed by the wide variety of activities they see happening in Great Commission outreach parishes. These leaders ask, "How can I dream up all these things?" They worry, "How will I manage all these activities?"

Leaders of Great Commission outreach congregations respond, "You are asking the wrong questions." The people God has blessed you with in your congregation will discover the ministry needs in the community.

The "priesthood of all believers" works in varied ways in Great Commission outreach congregations. For example, an electrician's mother moved from her home of fifty years to a retirement center. The house needed to be brought up to wiring codes before the buyer could get an FHA loan. The electrician discovered how dangerous his mother's home had been and reasoned that other older people in the community might have the same situation. He discussed this with other members, and before long three people started a rewiring ministry. Once a month they fix dangerous electrical problems in homes of elderly people.

In another parish, the treasurer was writing checks for church-sponsored teams in the community recreation league. The treasurer was checking the boys' basketball team roster to make sure the players were all church members. Then the treasurer thought, "That is a dumb rule for a congregation focused on reaching new members." The leadership took five minutes (not five months) to change the rule. Next season 20 percent of team members have to be people who do not belong to the congregation.

The most complex example of the "priesthood of all believers" involved a member who volunteered to help the congregation's music director and composer, who was being overwhelmed by requests for permission to use newly written music. The ten-hours-per-week volunteer position grew into a part-time job. The part-time position became full time. The full-time relationship grew into a publishing company. The publishing company expanded into consulting and staging conferences. The original volunteer ministry developed into a corporation that annually assists hundreds of ministries.

Congregations focused on ministry beyond current membership actively use the "priesthood of all believers." Their focus on unchurched people creates a vast number and variety of ministry opportunities for current members. Empowered members grow in their faith and service.

The spiritual needs of current members are met in new ways because these congregations focus on meeting needs of people.

Action Suggestion

Make a list of members already volunteering their skills for groups outside the congregation. Discuss with two of those members the possibility of their using their skills through the congregation.

Make another list of members who have skills needed by people in the community. Discuss with two members the possibility of their volunteering their skills to meet community needs through the congregation.

---

6. Outreach-focused congregations see clergy and laity as partners.

Clergy and laity work as partners in congregations with expanding ministry. They work together to establish the goals of the ministry. Clergy provide leadership, and laity conduct the ministries. High levels of trust are common in these congregations.

One pastor described this unique type of leadership. He said, "I realized something interesting about our ministry by accident. My daughter and I were picking up a book from my office on a Tuesday evening. We stopped to look at the posted list of that day's activities in the buildings. When my daughter asked about one activity, I told her I didn't know anything about it. Then it hit me. *It did not bother me that I didn't know about that activity.* I had never thought about it before. We trust each other here."

7. Outreach-focused congregations value "mistakes."

Congregations that are actively developing appropriate ways of working with their neighbors value learning from "mistakes." In fact, they do not make mistakes. Rather, they have ministries that do not develop as hoped. And they have no time for criticizing people who work with programs that have to be abandoned. The effort of these people is valued and the learning experience is appreciated.

This attitude is not found in parishes dominated by structural concerns. Such parishes are driven by churched-society attitudes that demand we work hard to *avoid* mistakes. Elaborate control systems assure that nothing happens unless everyone agrees. In particular, nothing happens unless the congregation's matriarch/patriarch approves—even if this historical leader has not held an elected position for many years. These congregations rarely try anything new because it is a disaster to make a mistake. They only do what has worked for years.

Action Suggestion

Make a list of congregation programs or activities that did not go well in the last three years. If there were none, discuss whether the congregation is looking hard enough to find ways to touch people. If there were some, ask the organizers of the activities how they were treated by other members before, during, and after the program developed problems.

---

8. Outreach-focused congregations care for people.

Caring for people is the heart of ministry beyond current members. Congregations that reach out are committed to the Christian faith as it is expressed in their denomination. However, they also recognize unchurched people are not seeking out theological positions. These congregations communicate their faith by being sensitive toward and acting to meet the needs of people in their neighborhood. They recognize that unchurched people are looking for places of healing and hope. They recognize that people join congregations, not denominations.

Ask yourself, "Why would an unchurched person come to our congregation?" Ask yourself, "Why would a person who gave up on organized religion many years ago return to our congregation?" In the churched society, a person would say, "I want to participate in the community of believers." In the unchurched society, the person looking for a church home says, "My life is not working and I need help."

Congregations respond in different ways to unchurched people who contact them. Congregations that touch the lives of large numbers of unchurched people recognize that love and caring, not theology and dogma, are needed. They adopt a host of behaviors to support caring ministry. They see caring ministry as following Jesus' example of touching the temporal and spiritual lives of people.

What Motivates Great Commission Congregations

Congregations that focus beyond current membership are not motivated by growth. They are motivated to reach people for Jesus. They achieve their Great Commission outreach goals in ways that make sense in the unchurched society. These congregations come in all shapes and colors—and sizes. Many small congregations have strong ministries. Many large parishes are slowly dying.

Senior pastors of the largest congregations that focus on reaching the unchurched never talk about growth as the goal. Growth is more often a difficult problem to handle. If growth occurs, it is a by-product of the ministry focus. One pastor of a five-campus congregation with 20,000 members describes the ministry in these terms.

"One day George called to say his friend Harry was in the hospital. George asked me to make a hospital call. I offered to help George make that call. George replied that I did not understand the request. But after additional conversation and encouragement, George agreed to work with me to learn how to make the hospital call. Two weeks later George called back. He described that hospital call as the hardest thing he had ever done in his life. Then George asked when he could do another one."

Another senior pastor describes his thoughts while driving to an elders' meeting after visiting a dying member. The visit had been an uplifting spiritual experience. The elders were going to be in their fifth hour of discussing whether the ushers should have badges. (If they had badges, should the ushers' name be engraved on the badge? If the name was engraved, should the ushers be allowed to take the badges home? If they took the badges home, what would happen when they forgot to bring their badges back?) The senior pastor was amazed at the difference between these two conversations and raised the issue with the elders. The elders agreed to swap ministries: The elders would become involved in important ministries and the staff would be trusted to decide about usher name badges and make other five-minute decisions.

The pastors of congregations focused on reaching unchurched people describe their congregations in terms of ministry to people. Growth is not the goal. If growth occurs, it is merely a side effect of focus on Great Commission outreach.

Expanding the Reach of Congregations

Congregations that reach out to people who are not yet members do so in many ways. They actively establish a variety of programs or activities that enable people to come into contact with the congregation. The monthly calendar of congregational activities is full of *entry points* for people who are not already members. They also have many social programs, presence outreach activities, but these congregations use their social ministries to make first-person contacts and to build relationships with people. In that way, their social service activities become Great Commission outreach ministries.

Many examples of entry points have been described in prior sections of this chapter. These are referred to as "side door" entry points. They are important. They are effective. They are not the most powerful.

The "front door" entry points are the congregation's regular worship opportunities. Congregations that reach out to the unchurched usually offer worship experiences that use more than one style of communication. Even outreach-oriented congregations with fewer than 100 people in worship each week offer more than one style of worship every week.

This concept will be discussed further in chapter 7.

> **Action Suggestion**
>
> The action suggestion on page 24 in chapter 4 is important. If you skipped the idea while reading chapter 4, complete the suggestion now: Examine two or three of your congregation's monthly calendars. Place a 1 by each listed activity that is designed for members only. Place a 2 by each activity that primarily supports the congregation's structure (choir, elders, finance, and so forth). Place a 3 by activities attended by large numbers of nonmembers. Share what you find with key leaders.

Igniter Events

Most congregations that currently focus on ministry beyond their current members experienced at some point in their history an *igniter event*: The congregation was in a period of stability or decline, then something significant happened, and their ministry was changed.

Igniter events can be positive. The ministry of a new pastor or active volunteer, completing a building expansion, receiving an unexpected bequest, or other uplifting events can ignite a congregation.

Igniter events can be negative. An indiscretion, fighting, membership loss, embezzlement, and a host of bad things can happen to congregations. When disaster strikes, most congregations decide to roll over and die. Some congregations decide, "We are sick and tired of being sick and tired."

One congregation experienced a true "igniter" event. Blockbuster Video built a huge store in front of their beautiful sanctuary. One night lightning struck the steeple, and the church burned to the ground. The congregation decided to rebuild behind Blockbuster Video. Why? Because everyone knows were the congregation is located. Who is "everyone"? All the current members. This congregation lost an opportunity because it focused on its current membership.

A pastor described moving from a large, active congregation to one with forty people in weekly worship. The four-person choir included two who could not carry a tune. The organist unsuccessfully tried to play like

a concert performer. After two weeks, the pastor discovered a group of
members was circulating petitions to remove the pastor. The next day the
little congregation's kitchen caught fire. After many prayers, and some
tears, the pastor and key leaders decided this congregation would focus
on ministry to the unchurched. Over the subsequent fifteen years the congregation started nine other congregations, grew to several thousand in
weekly worship attendance, and is moving from its crowded twenty-five-
acre campus to a two-hundred-acre site.

Igniter events have two common characteristics. First, they involve
large numbers of people. All leaders and a large portion of active members are affected. Long-range planning committee meetings or leadership
planning retreats are not igniter events.

Second, igniter events fundamentally alter how a congregation
thinks about its ministry. They cause the congregation to abandon
churched-society habits that no longer help ministry in the unchurched
society. Igniter events motivate members to become active disciples for
Christ rather than a passive audience that only hears about our Savior.
Igniter events enliven people for ministry beyond their current membership.

Whatever form an igniter event takes, however, only some congregations will respond positively to the wake-up call. Other congregations
will simply close, rather than reach out to the people God has given them
in their community.

For Reflection and Discussion

Identify the common characteristics of Great Commission, outreach-
focused congregations described in this chapter. How many of these
apply to your congregation or ministry?

*   Extend mission beyond current membership.

*   Seek local, contextual answers.

*   Meet people's needs, not needs of the organizational structural.

*   Organize around mission, not structure.

*   Use members' ministry gifts in new ministries.

*   See clergy and laity as partners.

*   Value "mistakes."

*   Care for people.

Identify specific people in your congregation who have skills that might help your congregation become known on the community grapevine as a center of healing and hope.

As you examine your congregation's ministry, remember that reaching people who are not already members requires a total congregational effort in a new direction. Be careful to avoid "magic pill" thinking, and avoid the temptation to start a new program to "save the congregation." Start by examining the central focus of God's church on earth.

CHAPTER 6

The Unchurched:
Who Are They?

The way you decide to approach unchurched people depends on your assumptions about the attitudes and interests of unchurched people. In the days of the churched culture, it was simple. All people of faith participated in a community of believers. Therefore, you could assume that an individual who was not a member of a congregation probably had little or no faith.

Congregations approached unchurched people by using any of a variety of methods to instill faith. Some approaches were aggressive, some more subtle. Most approaches centered on discussing with people the absence of God in their lives. The intent was to create in the unchurched an appreciation for the importance of faith.

A common approach was to provide the unchurched person with experiences that were profoundly moving to churched people. Churched people were moved by their favorite forms of worship, music, Bible stories, and other ways of communicating their beliefs. These experiences were so powerful to churched people that it was inconceivable to them that unchurched people would not feel the same way. If unchurched people chose not to join the church, churched people simply assumed these folks had hardened their hearts.

Some people were moved by these churchly forms of communication. The Holy Spirit found fertile ground for faith. Or at the very least, many people found faith after hearing the gospel through the communication form favored by churched people. This is not a criticism of the approaches used in the days of the churched society. It simply describes the church's treatment of unchurched people.

The "Effectively Unchurched"

Today roughly 50 percent of the people in the United States are effectively unchurched. "Effectively unchurched" means people do not participate in a congregation. Some effectively unchurched people do not claim membership in any congregation, and some claim membership in a congregation thousands of miles away. Some are on the membership roster of a congregation but do not attend very often. They might attend a major festival service once every third year. Researchers learned an interesting fact about these unchurched people. Most pollsters find 70 percent to 80 percent of effectively unchurched people say they have faith or that religion is important to their lives.

Researchers routinely find unchurched people report engaging in religious activity. Forty to 60 percent report praying to God daily or weekly, and 30 to 50 percent report reading the Bible regularly. Even if these numbers are a bit exaggerated, they are still impressive. These people claim faith. They simply choose not to participate in a local community of believers. (Some critics of these data contend that these unchurched "believers" fool themselves and that they are only politely giving courteous pollsters the "proper" answers.)

The idea of a "believing unchurched person" is a serious challenge for effective Great Commission outreach efforts. Working out of their own understanding of Gospel, church, and mission, churched people say to unchurched people, "Come to the church and be saved." However, unchurched people are not asking, "What must I do to be saved?" Rather, they ask "How can I make my life work?" In effect, people in the church are providing an answer to a question that unchurched people do not ask. (Whether or not the churched people are asking an important question is not relevant to the unchurched person's immediate concern.)

Unchurched people do not feel compelled to experience the worship life of a congregation when that worship experience does not communicate meaningfully with them. They do not feel compelled to participate in congregations simply out of a sense of responsibility.

Reasons for Leaving and Motivation to Return

Listening to formerly churched people talk about why they dropped out
of the church is a sobering experience. A group of formerly churched
people spent the first twenty minutes in a focus group getting to know
each other. Churched people observe the discussion from behind one-
way glass. The relaxed atmosphere abruptly changed when the moderator
said, "Tell me about what happened that caused you to drop out of your
last congregation."

The room became tense. People clenched the arms of their chair.
Lower lips started to quiver. Juggler veins began to pulse. With a tear in
her eye, a forty-year-old woman explained, "Fifteen years ago my brother
committed suicide." (The thought flashed through the observer's mind
that this happened fifteen years ago and she still exhibited an intense
physiological reaction!) "Fifteen years ago my brother committed suicide. The funeral sermon message was, 'This boy is in hell. Don't let this
happen to you.' Twenty-five people in my family became unchurched at
that instant."

Person after person went on to describe harsh treatment by their last
congregation. They described the full spectrum of life problems. One
after another, these former members related stories of hypocrisy, theological belligerence, sexual harassment, bias, and bigotry. In all cases, it
was overtly or subtly made clear to these people that they were not
wanted in the congregation. The observing churched people were very
embarrassed.

The truly scary part of the sessions came when the moderator asked,
"What should a congregation do to encourage you to return?" The actual
words used by these unchurched people when they replied were consis-
tent with most research on retrieving unchurched people. Unchurched
people described the importance of Scripture-based teachings, good
music, moving worship, and programs for children.

However, how the formerly churched answered was far more important than what they said. "Return to church. *(long pause)* That is an
interesting question. *(long pause)* I never really thought about that. *(long
pause)* I guess it should be Scripture-based. *(long pause and uncomfortable silence)* I suppose the music should be good. *(more uncomfortable
quiet)* I guess there should be good programs for children." It was clear
these people were politely answering a question calmly put to them by a

nice person in a safe environment. It was equally clear that they had no intention of giving organized religion another chance.

The comments of these unchurched people do not suggest that there is nothing congregations can do that will cause the unchurched to give church another chance. Death, disease, trauma, loneliness, pain, or other traumatic life events cause formerly churched people to give church another chance. When such things happen and a person looks to the church as a possible source of help, congregations then need to have high quality worship, music, Bible study, and programs. But life events, more than improved programs, are the powerful motivators that cause people to consider giving church another chance. (Of course, the next problem in reaching unchurched people is whether or not the congregation is an accepting, communicative, nurturing, and faith building experience.)

Action Suggestion

Count how many of the recent new members of your congregation were broken or hurting when they came to your congregation. If the answer is few or none, think about what that means to your congregation's ministry to the thousands of hurting people in your congregation's neighborhood.

Other Reasons for Leaving

The number of people who have experienced treatment that resulted in their dropping out of church is staggering. But 50 percent of formerly churched people dropped out simply when they moved away from the church they had been attending. Some church leaders have suggested a "moved member referral system" would be helpful. When a relocating member's name is sent to congregations in the new community, the receiving parish could then make contact with the new resident. Unfortunately, the few congregations that actively refer former members to congregations in their new communities tell a tragic tale: "We give the names of our former member to a congregation, but nothing happens."

Why should anything happen? Most congregations are primarily concerned about their current members. There is no strong reason to follow up on a new resident. After all, the congregation tried that once several years ago and the person did not join. The congregation does not want to make mistakes or to repeat a mistake made years ago.

Often lost in the discussion is the fact that 50 percent of formerly churched people dropped out of their congregations without moving. They simply drifted away. No one contacted 89 percent of these non-moving dropouts at the time they stopped participating in the congregation.

A staggering number of effectively unchurched people are baby boomers. In prior generations, most young people would drop out of the church and then return when they became parents, but only 50 percent of the 60 million baby boomers have come back. About 30 million boomers have dropped out of organized religion and have never come back. Now the scary part. These people are becoming grandparents. Their children and their grandchildren have never had any exposure to organized religion—except for occasional negative comments from their baby boomer relatives.

Another chilling reality of ministry with the formerly churched that is unexpected and of great concern is described by pastors in retirement communities in the southeast, Texas, the southwest, and the west coast: "People from up north are retiring to our communities. These retirees say they are 'retiring from work and the wars of the congregation.'" Clergy in these communities say ministry to migrating retired people is "harder than dealing with people who have never participated." At least "never-evers" do not have to overcome harsh treatment by other congregations.

After They're in the Door

Congregations that seek to reach unchurched people, whatever the people's reasons for being unchurched, realize it is not possible to communicate with people who are ignoring your existence. These congregations utilize all available front-door, back-door, and side-door points of entry, as many methods of making contact as they can dream up.

After making contact with a nonmember, however, another issue is raised. In the churched culture, most people knew what a congregation was and how it worked. People would participate in a new member class, where they learned or reviewed basic teachings and a few important congregational procedures. People were asked to attest to those teachings publicly, probably at a worship service. There might have been a meal for new members. Then the new members had to find their own way in the congregation. Most did just fine. If they eventually left, that was all right. Members thought the new person probably did not belong in that congregation in the first place.

The unchurched culture creates a very different situation. Some unchurched people have no church background whatever. Others have to overcome negative treatment received in another congregation. Most congregations reaching large numbers of unchurched people use an intentional approach to integrating new members. One integration process is called the "Circle of Fulfillment." A sequence of four courses replaces the traditional one-course approach.

The basic course is "Discover the Congregation." Many new members have no idea what a congregation is or how it operates. Even the "obvious" concept that members financially support the ministry is new, and new members have no idea how congregations make decisions. They need, and receive, explanation about the congregation.

"Discover Maturity in Faith" is similar to new member classes in most congregations. People come to a congregation, not to a theology, so they know little about the congregation's teaching. In this second course, the beliefs and fundamental teachings of the congregation are explained. Most congregations begin and end with this course, but the outreach-oriented congregation does not stop where most congregations stop.

The third course is called "Discover Ministry to Others." Faith is not something to be kept inside the individual. All congregations tell people to live out their faith. This congregation takes the time to help people feel the need to take action.

The fourth course is "Discover Mission in Our Backyard and Around the World." This course helps the new member to select a ministry, to go beyond "having" faith. The course helps people live out their faith.

Action Suggestion

Examine the content of your new member course. What are new members asked to do when the course is completed? Are they asked to "become a member" and join an audience to hear the Good News? Are they assisted in identifying a specific ministry in which they can become personally involved to respond to the Good News?

For Reflection and Discussion

In the churched society, congregations took a lot for granted about unchurched people. For the times, that approach worked. In the unchurched society, efforts to reach unchurched people are completely different.

Examine the possibility of gathering and listening to a group of unchurched people who live near your congregation. List the topics you would like to hear them discuss. Identify someone in your area who has skills at asking questions and the patience to draw out answers, who would be willing to be the discussion leader. In larger communities, an experienced focus group moderator will probably be available. In almost all communities, a person trained in counseling, psychology, social work, or similar professions will be available and happy to help.

Before actually carrying out this idea, be sure you are willing to listen to (and not argue about) some challenging opinions.

CHAPTER 7

Worship Style:
A Lightning-Rod Issue

The way congregations worship has become a lightning-rod issue in most discussions about reaching unchurched people. The discussion generates fire and heat. The impact of worship on people, however, is substantial and cannot be ignored. Worship is the most potent activity of congregations. Side-door entry points are important, but the front-door entry point of the weekly worship experience is far more powerful because worship is a mirror to the rest of the congregation. What happens in worship reflects what happens in teaching, social activities, meetings, and the rest of that complex mix of interactions that is a congregation.

Most denominational traditions have one general method of conducting congregational worship. This method, with a few variations, is usually called "traditional." For most mainline Protestant denominations and the Catholic church, traditional worship is a form with European roots.

In some traditions, the specific words used in worship have become as important as the intended message, and suggestions to use different words are treated as an attack on the sanctity of the denomination's beliefs. The method of communicating theology becomes tightly wrapped around the underlying theology. In fact, in some cases, the wrapper is so tight that it is not possible to separate the method of communication from the underlying beliefs. Pseudotheology is created. "Pseudotheology" is a variety of thoughts, words, concepts, opinions, procedures, and habits that are treated as if they are the source theology.

In the churched culture, congregations within a denomination were similar to each other. The method of communicating a denomination's theology could be identical in all congregations within that denomination. A goal of denominational hymnal projects was to ensure that everyone would have the same worship experience in each of the denomination's congregations. The liturgy and hymnology were structured, taught, and practiced as if they were the only proper way to communicate the denomination's underlying theology. Pseudotheology was created around worship style.

Changing Rules

The unchurched culture has changed the rules for congregations that seek to respond to the Great Commission. Now each congregation is on a unique mission field. Methods of communicating the theological principles held by the congregation must fit the particular mission field. Some people accept this assertion. Others are appalled.

People steeped in their denomination's traditional forms of worship find those forms very meaningful. The number of these people in congregations is large. The percentage of these people in congregations is very large. However, both the numbers and percentages are shrinking.

Many people, especially baby boomers, do not find traditional forms of worship very meaningful. Two facts are important. First, the 30 million boomers who did not return to church, plus their children and now their grandchildren, constitute a very large group of effectively unchurched people. Second, this is not an age issue. Every congregation that has started some alternate form of worship "for the young people" has expressed amazement at the large number of older people who attend. Traditional forms of worship do not touch the spiritual lives of a growing number and percentage of people.

Most discussions about worship style degenerate into divisive and unhealthy "either/or" arguments. Churched-culture congregations define themselves as a place where "we worship together using a single form of communication." There is no room for "both/and" thinking. Resolution of the issue is not easy and typically does not result from debates among liturgical experts or in heated congregational meetings. Resolution actually happens in quiet moments of understanding. Two incidents are typical.

Members of a congregation listened to a Sunday afternoon presentation about declining church membership. The presenter asked the members to offer their views on the causes. George rose to speak and a hush fell over the room. Everyone was listening. In front of the whole congregation and with a tear in his eye, George said, "The hardest thing in my life is that my thirty-seven-year-old son will not bring my twelve-year-old grandson to worship and Sunday school."

Two hours later the presenter described current realities about worship style, liturgy, and hymnology. George again rose to speak. The room again became quiet but in a different way. George was very agitated. Using firm tones, George asserted, "The way we worship in this congregation is so rich and meaningful to me, I cannot see how anyone else would not feel the same way. We must conduct worship the way we have always done it in this congregation."

The room atmosphere was thick with controversy. Members sat in silence. What would happen next? The speaker said nothing. George did not sit down. George did not speak. The frowning expression on George's face changed. He had that look of insight in his eye, like when a small child suddenly understands how to tie a shoe. A light bulb had just come on. George said nothing further, sat down, and the presentation continued.

One month later, George was observed leaving a workshop on high quality, nontraditional worship. George described his light-bulb experience: "I realized I was holding the spiritual development of my grandson hostage to my personal preference for a certain form of communication in worship. I realized that thousands of people in our community would be 'left out' if we insist on using only one form of communication. I realized that millions of people in our world will be 'left out' if we insist on using only one form to communicate the Good News."

A second incident was very private. A woman had attended a presentation about the value of being open-minded about worship style. At another meeting six weeks later she explained, "My daughter is going to marry a nice Christian man from a different denomination. They will be worshiping using a style with which I am not comfortable. I was angry with my daughter for falling away from the true expression of faith, and I estranged myself from her for almost a year. I cannot tell you how grateful I am for seeing how wrong I have been. Jesus never dictated any particular form of worship. Why should I be so presumptuous as to denigrate a form of worship just because I am not able to appreciate it for myself?"

Adding a New Style of Communication

Offering more than one style of worship is an excellent strategy for ministry beyond current membership. Congregations that have followed this approach find that adding a new style of worship is like starting a new congregation. They offer six suggestions:

1. Do not start by saying, "We need a contemporary service." Instead, start by asking, "Which group of people in our neighborhood would we like to reach." The focus is on ministry, not music.

2. Find out how to communicate with these people. This means visiting them—in a personal way, not an institutional manner. Do not gather current members around a table to exchange a few anecdotes, hearsay, and misinformation. Conduct one-on-one or small group discussions in which the congregation's neighbors do most of the talking and the members mostly listen.

3. Empower a mission team to create the service. Authorize the group to do the necessary research and to make the service happen. Rather than seeking approval from the existing structure, trust fellow members to do what is right. Empowerment is not possible in structure-dominated congregations that are unwilling to acknowledge the un-churched society.

The "mission team" empowered to create the new service needs to be made up of people committed to Great Commission outreach and to quality presentation. People committed to the traditional methods will not be helpful. At least half the mission team should be from the target group for whom the new worship service is intended. Most people whose expertise is only in traditional worship forms will not be helpful. People who already have new skills, or who are willing to learn, should be the clear majority of members of these action teams.

4. Determine the style of worship—including music, congregational singing, liturgy, Bible reading, preaching, and prayer—for the new service after completing the first three steps. This is easy when a large portion of mission team members are from the target group. When no one from the target group is on the mission team, selecting a communication style will be fraught with missteps, which give detractors opportunity to say "I told you so."

5. Remember, this is a matter of both/and, not either/or. The congregation has many fine Christian people who appreciate the traditional

ways of doing things. Traditional forms of communication in worship are wonderful, meaningful, and important, and they need to continue. One transition strategy is to keep the traditional services at their current times. The form of worship communication being introduced will often be most effective when it does not replace an existing service.

People who operate congregations under the rules of the churched culture will have difficulty dealing with this type of arrangement. Their experience is that congregations only have unity when all members all do everything the same way. When member disagree, their congregational history dictates that members fight until one group quits talking or leaves the congregation. These people are not able to see the unity of Great Commission outreach that lies at the heart of worship communication-style diversity.

6. Some congregations seek to resolve the dispute by using several types of communication in the same service. This compromise is called "blended worship." Blended worship is a style unique to itself. In some congregations it is very effective. In other congregations, it simply means that by the end of the service everyone has been offended at least once.

Some congregations seek resolution by *rotating* worship styles each Sunday. Normally this approach creates confusion because people do not remember which form of communication is used which Sunday. This approach seems to work only in a few situations.

The Language of the Unchurched

Congregations committed to reaching unchurched people are open to different ways of communicating their beliefs. They know it is possible to preserve the unchangeable substance of their faith while speaking to the unchurched in the language of the unchurched.

One congregation speaks in five "languages" in weekend worship services. The Sunday morning service at 8:00 a.m. is in "traditional" language. Liturgy is from the denomination's official hymnal. Men wear suits or sport coats and ties. Women wear dresses and skirts. The 9:00 a.m. service uses "spirited traditional" language. The order of service is fairly traditional, but the music is more up-tempo. Most men wear ties, but very few wear suits or sport coats. "High energy participative" language is spoken at 10:00 a.m. Some refer to this as a contemporary service. Nobody wears a necktie. The 11:00 a.m. service is "rock and roll," and the Good News Band leads the music. Some people wear tank tops, T-shirts, and shorts. The Saturday evening service is country western. People wear plaid shirts, blue jeans held up by belts with huge buckles, and even cowboy boots.

The differences between the "messages" (sermons) at the five services are fascinating. Three pastors use the same text but a variety of methods of exploring it. Each message is tailored to the type of person at the particular service. The pastor who leads the traditional service is not allowed anywhere near the country western service. The traditional-service pastor explains, "I do not know how to say 'yahoo' correctly." The country-western service pastor interrupts to point out, "We do not say 'yahoo' anymore. Now we say 'yee-ha.'"

People raised in the churched society typically have two problems with this strategy of using different languages for different worship services. First, they are offended that people attend worship wearing less than their "Sunday best." They do not want to worship next to people dressed so "disrespectfully." But leaders of the congregation point out, "What choice do we have? Do we prefer these people to stay home? What would Jesus say about how people are dressed? How people are dressed has nothing whatever to do with communicating the saving message of Jesus."

The second problem raised by churched-society people is more a mystery than a problem. These people cannot understand how several groups of people can coexist in the same congregation. These people were trained to fight about preferences until one point of view wins. Winning means people who lose the argument leave the congregation.

In contrast, congregations committed to Great Commission outreach in the unchurched society are comfortable with the reality of delivering an unchanging message in a wide variety of ways. Great Commission outreach congregations celebrate these differences as a means to enlarge the kingdom. Different preferences are never considered divisive but are celebrated because through them a variety of people are reached.

Some congregations cite another concern. They say, "We are not big enough to have that kind of variety." Congregations of all sizes, however, are able to use more than one style of communication in worship. The "five languages" congregation did not start big. In fact, fifteen years ago it had eighty members, with forty in weekly worship, and a choir of four people, only two of whom could carry a tune. A North Carolina congregation with 300 in weekly worship has an 8:00 a.m. "Gospel" service, a 9:15 a.m. "contemporary, family" service, and 10:30 a.m. "liturgical" service. Worship attendance is increasing weekly. A rural Idaho congregation had fifty people in worship. They now have 150 attending either the "heritage" service or the "celebration" service.

The Real Issue

I want to close this chapter on worship style with an outrageous statement. Despite the fury of the discussion on this topic, worship style is not the main point. Debate about worship style deals with a symptom, not the main problem. The real issue is openness. More specifically, the issue is openness to Great Commission outreach ministry. Congregations with closed attitudes about worship style also have closed attitudes about almost everything else. Congregations that are not willing to consider alternate forms of communicating unchangeable truth are also not open to the variety of people in their God-given, neighborhood mission field.

To repeat a critical point, debates about worship style, hymnology, and liturgy are really *debates about whether or not the congregation will be in mission to more than its current members.*

For Reflection and Discussion

Search the Gospels and locate all the passages where Jesus

* listed the styles of music required for worship

* described the appropriate forms of liturgy for worship

* explained the appropriateness of dress for worship

Without making any final decisions or commitments, discuss the following four questions:

* Who in our congregation's neighborhood are we not reaching?

* How could we arrange to visit with several of these people?

* If we empowered a mission team to create a new service, who would be on that team?

* Are we open to reaching our neighbors if that means holding an additional worship service using a different style of worship?

CHAPTER 8

Ideas That Do Not Automatically Work

Some solutions to membership problems turned out to be only partially helpful. Once we find a partially helpful answer, we need to decide how aggressively to pursue that line of thinking. Partially helpful answers are useful to some people and a waste of time to others. The following three sections describe outreach ideas that are not as helpful as we might expect.

New Members Studies

Discovering why new members have joined a congregation can be helpful in comparison with *theorizing* about why people will join. People join congregations, not denominations. Unchurched people join because of family reasons or because a friend invites them. Very few people join today because of the kind of evangelism programs and methods used in the days of the churched society. People join because characteristics of the congregation match what they seek.

Discovering why new members join a congregation is only half the information needed to understand why people join. The other half is why visitors *do not* join the congregation. Unfortunately, we know very little about this critical aspect of outreach.

Congregations would do well to contact visitors who do not return. Because few people will risk being offensive by being honest about their concerns, however, congregations should listen to but basically ignore visitors' polite answers. Instead, find out where these nonreturning visitors are worshiping six months after visiting your congregation. Compare the congregation they join with your congregation. That comparison will tell you more about your Great Commission outreach opportunities than will discussions with new members.

Parochial Schools as Outreach

Some congregations operate or affiliate with a day-care program or school of some type (preschool, elementary school, high school). All these congregations refer to the school as their "outreach to the community." Pastors and school principals frequently encourage unchurched parents to participate in the congregation's life.

The school's relationship to congregational membership falls into three general categories.

1. Some congregations experience membership gains from the school, as well as gains from other sources. The school is part of an overall Great Commission outreach ministry.

2. For some congregations, their only new members come from the school. This is particularly true when parents are required to join the congregation so their children can attend the school.

3. Some congregations are not experiencing any membership gains of any type, despite the presence of the school. The school is an example of presence outreach that does not result in Great Commission outreach. This situation is dangerous for the congregation and the school. The danger for the congregation is that it thinks maintaining the school fulfills the congregation's Great Commission outreach in the unchurched society.

The danger for the school is that it thinks Great Commission outreach is the responsibility of the school. Nothing the school does, however, can overpower the visible and invisible barriers the congregation has erected. Eventually the school will be blamed for the congregation's lack of new members, although the problem is in the congregation: The congregation remains focused on ministry to current members. The congregation grows weaker, and the school is labeled an albatross and closed. There are a few exceptions where the school is able to charge sufficient tuition to be financially independent. More commonly, however, the congregation remains focused on current members until the last member moves away or dies. As the parish shrinks, income necessary to subsidize the school drops. The school is closed "to save the congregation," and in a few years, or decades, the parish will also close.

New Church Planting

Everyone's data say the same thing: New congregations bring the largest proportion of new members into a denomination. Starting new congregations is an important method of reaching beyond current membership.

Within this truth lie three realities and one dilemma. First, most new congregations start small and stay small. During the days of the churched society, a new parish would be planted in a wheat field on the outskirts of a town or city. Twenty years later the congregation was large and financially strong. Denominational loyalty, population mobility, birth rate, and the rubric that "grandparents would roll over in their graves if we did not attend church" created growing congregations. These powerful attributes have been greatly diminished in the unchurched society.

Second, starting small congregations as the primary means of growing denominations can be horribly expensive. This is particularly true in denominations that start congregations by hiring full-time workers, buying land, and constructing buildings. (One denomination's current practice of starting congregations that stay small will require $1.4 billion to recover the 500,000 members lost since 1970.) A new model for establishing new congregations is needed. Some people suggest the new model should be for existing congregations to take responsibility for new church planting.

Third, using existing congregations as the primary vehicle for church planting sounds good—but there is one key problem. Most congregations in most denominations are weak and getting weaker. Denominations are no stronger than the collective strength of their individual congregations. Most denominations have very few congregations strong enough to plant the number of congregations needed to offset what is being lost by weak congregations.

These three realities, together with the fact that resources are limited, lead to a serious dilemma. Should dwindling resources be poured into starting new congregations? Should dwindling resources be invested in strengthening existing congregations so that more resources will become available for future church planting? If both strategies are appropriate, what is the proper balance between them?

Ultimately, however, the question is whether large numbers of congregations can accomplish what has been impossible. Is it possible to enliven internally focused congregations effectively to reach beyond their

current membership? Books like the one you are reading attempt to be
helpful. It is even more helpful to study and pray about these issues with
other church leaders.

For Reflection and Discussion

Think about the history of your congregation. Was there a time when
members were actively reaching new people? (Actively reaching new
people is not the same as passively signing up people from other places
who happened to be moving into the neighborhood.) Specifically what
was happening then in the congregation and neighborhood during that
time? Has that Great Commission outreach activity continued into the
present? If not, can the magic of that past excitement be awakened?

CHAPTER 9

Seven Words Say It All

The project responsible for generating this large body of information intended to find solutions to the problem of declining membership. All the research, time, and resources led to a simple idea. Solutions to most church problems lie within

individual, motivated congregations taken one at a time.

Individual

Denominations are no stronger than the collective strength of their individual congregations. Membership problems in denominations will only be solved when large numbers of individual congregations successfully address local membership issues. Denominational money problems can only be solved when individual congregations understand that "money follows mission." Solutions to most problems in the church will only come when many individual congregations become stronger.

Motivated

Congregations grow weaker or stronger depending on their central focus. Most congregations that focus exclusively on current members slowly grow weaker. Some people have suggested that congregations that ignore nonmembers in their neighborhoods have decided to die. The only question is, when will death occur?

Congregations motivated to reach people who are not currently members find ways to grow stronger. Their motivation to respond to our Lord's Great Commission is the key. The intensity of their motivation makes the difference.

Great Commission outreach congregations understand two critical points. First, growth and size are not the issue. The issue is the central focus of the ministry. Growth and size are side effects of ministry and may or may not happen. They are measures of effectiveness, not the target goals.

Second, regional and national offices can be helpful. However, no amount of help from denominations will make much difference if congregations do not view themselves as the responsible parties. Congregations waiting for regional or national activities to solve congregational problems will still be waiting when the congregation closes.

Taken One at a Time

Pigeonholing congregations creates problems. Negative reactions to congregational classification schemes are understandable. On the other hand, people in individual congregations find that general classifications help them see at least some implications of their congregation's actions. Differences in congregations' attitudes about Great Commission outreach result in three general classifications, which have been helpful to individual congregations and are useful in generating discussion about ministry focus.

Group A congregations are organized to reach new people. They intentionally include people who are not already members, and they continue to do excellent work to meet needs of current members. Group A congregations work to be more effective at Great Commission outreach. Some Group A congregations actively help other congregations learn about being effective.

Group B1 congregations are interested in reaching people who are not currently members. However, they are having a difficult time letting go of their churched-society habits. They still practice time-honored traditions known to be barriers to outsiders. Group B1 congregations are looking for ways to be more like Group A congregations.

Group B2 congregations define themselves in terms of their current members. They cannot conceive of changing anything. They are *firmly*, exclusively committed to their current members. They comfort themselves with statements such as, "Anyone is welcome." This phrase consciously or subconsciously concludes "...as long as they do things the way we do them." Group B2 congregations are not interested in changing.

Principles for Congregational Change

Group B1 congregations recognize the need to change. They find it difficult to change. Although we know little about the congregation change or transition process, a few principles are clear.

1. *Knowledge* of the need for change must precede attitude change. Many members are only vaguely aware of the congregation's weak record of Great Commission outreach. Most members are not aware of their parish's membership, worship attendance, and other indicators of possible problems. Problems experienced by visitors are invisible to current members. Most members do not mean to offend visitors, even though offense is frequently taken. Simply informing members of the impact of their actions is a necessary first step.

2. *Attitude change* must precede behavior change. After understanding how time-honored activities cause outreach problems, some members say, "So what?" People who feel the congregation exists solely to meet their preferences are not open to behavior change. These people have no motivation to change attitudes or behaviors. Fortunately, most members feel at least a general responsibility to follow the Great Commission. They are willing to listen further. They are open to becoming motivated to think about behavior change.

3. *Individual behavior change* comes before organizational behavior change. Congregational programs to open up the ministry are useless when members choose to retain their closed habits. When individual members decide to act differently, the parish is ready to change its collective behavior.

4. *Organizational behavior change* is complex. At a 1994 Leadership Network meeting, Ken Blanchard pointed out some interesting numbers. When two people interact, there are two relationships. When three people interact, there are twelve potential relationships, not nine, as most

people expect. (The extra three sets of interactions occur because the third person may or may not be present.) When four people interact, there are fifty-four possible relationships. In a group the size of a congregation, organizational behavior is very complex.

5. Organizations looking for collective group behavior change can only absorb a *limited number of changes* at one time. Leaders must limit themselves to a manageable number of changes. Pursuing more than three to five changes at one time is too much for complex organizations to handle. Enthusiastic leaders frequently overload the congregation and create resistance.

6. People come to discussions about change with *different perspectives* and consequently often end up talking past each other. In order to have discussions that are genuinely helpful, it is important for all parties to begin by recognizing the value of the perspectives that others bring.

A particularly clear demonstration of this principle occurred in a conversation between a congregation's new music director and the senior pastor. The formerly strong congregation was in a deteriorating neighborhood. Most members had left the community and the congregation. For a variety of reasons, the choir had become disorganized and frequently sang off-tune. A new director had been hired following the accidental death of the long-term music leader. (The senior pastor was out of the country on an archeological sabbatical and could not be contacted, and the congregation wanted a replacement immediately, so the director had been hired without discussion with the senior pastor.)

At the first service following the senior pastor's return, the choir beautifully sang a time-honored, favorite hymn. The pastor was impressed. At last they had an excellent choir, much like they had in the good ol' days. Later in the service the choir offered a medley of three hymns that used a rock-and-roll tempo. A few neighborhood people on the corner outside heard the music and wandered into the sanctuary. Many of those in attendance seemed pleased. The senior pastor was furious. A heated exchange occurred between the senior pastor and the music director.

At various points during the exchange, the new music director offered the following comments:

"I was thinking more like a concert. You know? Get some people in here."

"You see, people like going to concerts, but they do not like coming to church. Why? Because church is dull. But we could change all that."

"We could jam this place."

"We could bring this place alive."

The senior pastor was outraged and reacted accordingly to the director's attempt to add a new musical style of communication to the congregation's worship service.

"Rock and roll on a piano. What were you thinking?"

"And what next? Dancers? This is not a theater for rock concerts."

"We will not reach people through blasphemy!"

The exchange was frustrating and deadlocked. Both people were using language that was offensive to the other, and both were ignoring the appropriate concerns of the other. The senior pastor sought to be responsive to the *churched society*. The music director sought to be responsive to the *mission field* in which the congregation is now located. The pastor sought to preserve the effective traditions from the churched society. The music director sought to reach out to new people with a new language.

Both the music director and the pastor are dedicated people of God, eager to be faithful to their ministry—as they understand that ministry. Unfortunately, this exchange is all too typical of the "debates" that go on in congregations. Some people are enthusiastic about the opportunity for an exciting new ministry. They promote "new language for new people," and in the process offend others. At the same time, others feel responsible for "protecting" or at least dealing with members of the congregation who are not ready for change. They prefer the congregation to be a place of rest, comfort, and safety.

Of course, communication is always a two-way process, and both the pastor and the music director must take responsibility for their poor communication. But no matter how we view this exchange, we can no doubt see the value of another way of handling it. Just as the pastor was about to fire the choir director, the congregation's president entered and took a quite different approach:

"I haven't enjoyed services this much in a very long time."

"What marvelous music. Innovative. Inspiring."

"I can't wait until next Sunday when the choir sings again."

"Did you see the people walk right in from the street?"

"That music called to them."

The focus of the conversation changed dramatically. The president recognized the pastor's perspective and the discussion no longer focused on worship style. Rather, it shifted to ministry objectives. The chances are much better that future discussions will focus on ministry, not music. (Even when all concerned are able to communicate clearly and respectfully, however, it is not easy to discuss changes in worship style with people still living as if the congregation were in a churched culture. And ultimately, outreach programs do not work when inserted in congregations where the leaders and members are not committed to Great Commission outreach.)

7. It is helpful is to recognize the *thought sequence* through which individuals and congregations pass as they begin to realize the future is not like the past. Members and congregations start at different places and proceed at different paces through this sequence.

Becoming a Great Commission outreach congregation means leaders and a large portion of the members need to

* realize there is a problem;

* accept the fact that the world has changed;

* see clearly the difference between internal and external focus;

* decide that the congregation can achieve Great Commission out reach.

8. *Assistance is available* to congregations that understand the four points listed above. Printed materials, video instruction, conferences, workshops, consultants, and denominational resources are available everywhere. High quality resources on change, leadership development, mission growth, evangelism, worship, strategic planning, computer demographics, and many other helpful topics are available. A few denominations and publishers have assembled collections of these resources. Some regional offices can provide people who help congregations access these sources.

The most helpful source of information will be congregations that are already achieving Great Commission outreach in a community similar to your congregation's. Although these field-based experts may or may not be members of the same denomination as your congregation's, they will be happy to share what they have learned.

9. *Patience* is necessary. Laying foundations before introducing

change is important. New ideas take time to sink in. One or two enthusiastic leaders are not enough. Small-group and one-on-one discussions about transitions are more helpful than strong pronouncements that create winners and losers.

For Reflection and Discussion

Think about your current ministry.
How many people realize there is a problem?
How many people accept that the world has changed?
How many people clearly see the difference between internal and external focus in ministry?
How many people believe your congregation can carry out Great Commission outreach?

CHAPTER 10

The Changed Society: How It Affects the Church

Differences of opinion abound about how the church relates to society. Most differences stem from the fact that our society has changed—from churched to unchurched. Both sides are correct—from their different underlying perspectives. But when people start from different assumptions, they talk past each other. Everyone expresses their own opinions. Everyone leaves the discussion convinced they are correct and wondering how the others can be so wrong.

This chapter returns to the format used in chapter 1. It presents sixteen additional transitions that show how the change from a churched society to an unchurched society directly impacts congregations and those attempting to help congregations. Some of the most important examples for previous chapters have been repeated here as a reminder and even a prod: "This is what needs to be changed in our ministry on Monday."

Congregational Transitions

The eight congregational transitions described here are caused by the shift from a churched society to an unchurched society. They were discovered by comparing struggling congregations with thriving congregations.

Most congregations still operate as if they existed in a churched society. When many of them describe their desired future, they express longing for a return to the way things were ten, twenty, thirty, forty, or more years ago. Some think working with or adapting to these transitions compromises their theology. They see congregations as places of refuge from the ravages of all the changes.

Most thriving congregations in the unchurched society have found ways to work with the transitions. They see their future in terms of harnessing new strengths while they carefully abandon failing activities. They view emerging realities as "ministry challenges to be confidently overcome."

Transition 8: Congregations focus beyond current membership.

In the churched society, congregations were predominantly made up of people who had been members for many years. Newer members generally came from other congregations, usually congregations in the same denomination. Clergy and members enjoyed being among people who were familiar with Bible stories, the progression of the church year, liturgy, common hymns, and the central aspects of their faith. They found comfort in reminding themselves of these familiar expressions of their faith.

The customs and practices of these long-term members supported strong bonds of membership. Individuals who transferred to another parish within a denomination participated in virtually the same activities. The time-tested programs used for decades were the strength and stability of the local gathering of believers.

Most members support virtually all activities of churched society congregations. It was unusual for any activity to occur unless most members had agreed to it. The members worked hard to conduct programs of interest to current members. They encouraged current members to participate in all activities.

Meeting the needs and interests of current members was the basis for all decisions. Anyone else could participate, as long as these new people completely accepted the methods, procedures, and activities of the current members.

In the unchurched society, sensitivity to characteristics of unchurched people is necessary. Most visitors and new members are not familiar with common Bible stories, liturgy, hymns, or most other aspects of faith. The familiar expressions of faith continue to be a comfort to long-term members. These same expressions of faith are practiced in ways that help unchurched people receive help and comfort.

The customs and practices of long-term members are supported. At the same time, new traditions are established. Time-tested programs yielding desired results are continued. New ideas with potential for a-chieving new goals are attempted. People who transferred from another congregation in the same denomination continue to see the fundamentals of their denomination. Transferees also experience new ways to reach broken and hurting people with a healing Jesus.

Many activities are developed specifically to reach people who are not already members. Activities are effectively advertised to the general public, as well as to the members. Reaching out to people who are not already members becomes a major focus of the congregation. Not only are new people welcome, they are actively sought.

Think about your current congregation or ministry situation. List the specific ways nonmembers actively participate.

_____

_____

_____

_____

_____

TRANSITION 9: **Congregations defend the faith by proclaiming the faith.**

Congregations in the churched society developed many time-honored ways of explaining their beliefs. Great care was taken over the decades to screen what was acceptable from what was not. Individual words in liturgies, hymns, and other forms of communication were scrutinized. Highly emotional loyalty developed for these sacred traditions.

The method of communicating theological positions became heavily intertwined with statements of belief. Suggestions to modify the prac-tices, or even individual words, led to theological investigations, and emo-tions ran high. Most suggestions for modifying practice and procedure were treated as threats to the denomination's basic beliefs. People offering suggestions were treated harshly. Many congregations found themselves spending large amounts of time defending their faith against the onslaught of new and unfamiliar ideas.

Congregations in the unchurched society find that many of the time-tested practices do not provide the same levels of comfort and hope as they once did, and that sometimes new people have preferences that do not match preferences of long-term members.

The help and hope offered in Scripture are not tied to specific methods of communicating those truths. And the unchurched society wants to hear faith and salvation proclaimed in familiar terms. Congregations in the unchurched society acknowledge that firm and clear belief statements do not have to be tied to specific words and phrases that were developed by different people in different times.

The unchurched society seeks ministry that uses methods and procedures appropriate to the people being addressed by each individual ministry. Some traditional approaches are abandoned, other traditions are retained, and newer approaches are added. The principal difference is that churches in the unchurched society have tolerance for more than one method of communicating the unchanging truths contained in the Holy Scriptures.

Responding to the realities of the unchurched society means becoming clear about what is sacred (unchangeable) and what is tradition (appropriate to the times).

Estimate the number of hours the congregation you attend spends proclaiming the faith to current members. Estimate the number of hours it spends proclaiming the faith to people not already members—*using communication methods appropriate to those nonmembers.*

_____

_____

_____

_____

_____

TRANSITION **10: Unchurched people have faith.**

Transition 2 described the relationship between faith and congregational members in the churched society. People of faith would *automatically* participate with the community of believers. People of faith would not think of dropping out of a congregation—regardless of how bad things might have become in their congregation. This powerful reality meant that anyone who was not already a congregation member must, by definition, be a person without faith. Thus, efforts to reach unchurched people centered on lack of faith.

Some congregations used their beliefs about faith to explain why they were not responsible for Great Commission outreach. They believed the Holy Spirit works faith in the hearts of people. The congregation only needed to teach and preach properly. The Holy Spirit chose to bless or not bless the congregation numerically. The parish was not responsible for reaching nonmembers. To suggest that congregational activities have a major role to play in outreach was to question teachings about the Holy Spirit.

In the unchurched society, millions of people have separated faith from congregation participation. Some people dropped out of congregations because the time-honored methods demanded by current members had no meaning for them. Some were driven out by congregations that concentrated on defending the faith against all new ideas. Many younger people do not participate because their baby boomer parents and grandparents dropped out decades before.

About three-quarters of effectively unchurched people in the United States claim some level of faith. Over half of the these people indicate some form of prayer life. Churched people often say, "Return and be saved." However, unchurched people ask, "How can I make my life work?"

The local congregation must find effective ways to communicate with unchurched people. Finding effective ways of getting people's attention means accepting people as they are.

Does your congregation desire to come into contact with unchurched people? If so, do large numbers of unchurched people come around often enough to hear the saving message you offer?

_____

_____

_____

_____

_____

TRANSITION 11: Joining a congregation is a six-step process.

In the churched society, all we did was install a congregation and people would join. Denominational loyalty was high. For several centuries, boat loads of people immigrated to this country. They formed or joined congregations of the same denomination as their ancestors's churches. After World War II, a huge number of children were born in families who stayed in their ancestral denomination. When people relocated, they sought a congregation in the denomination of their ancestors.

In the churched culture, persuading people to join a congregation was a two-step process. Step one was to make people aware the congregation existed. Step two was to sign people into membership. No special effort was needed to contact nonmembers. Very few changes were made to accommodate the wishes of nonmembers. After a relatively short new member class, the recent additions were left on their own.

In some traditions, the two-step process demonstrated a core belief of the denomination: A congregation merely needs to teach properly and leave the rest to the Holy Spirit.

How people choose a congregation is different in the unchurched society. Denominational loyalty is low. Large numbers of immigrants have stopped coming from Europe. Current members are dying or leaving much faster than current members are marrying or giving birth to new members. When they move, people no longer aggressively seek a congregation of their heritage.

George Hunter's book How to Reach Secular People *masterfully describes how unchurched people find healing and hope in a congregation.[1] A six-step process has replaced the two-step process of the churched society.*

*   *People need to be* aware *the congregation exists.*

*   *People need to see that the congregation is* relevant *to their lives.*

*   *Only then might they develop an* interest *in exploring the congregation.*

*   *People tentatively* explore *the congregation through trial participation.*

*   *They might* adopt *the congregation as their own by joining.*

*   *Even after joining, they need* reinforcement *for their joining.*

Reaching new people in the unchurched society involves significantly more effort than in the churched society. More thought and programming are necessary when inexperienced people affiliate with a congregation.

What does the congregation you attend do differently than it did ten years ago to touch the lives of people who are not now members?

_____

_____

_____

_____

_____

TRANSITION 12: **Worship attendance and the number of people served, not membership, tells the story.**

Membership was the most important congregational statistic in the churched culture. People compared numbers of members to see who was doing better. Each year, clergy looked in the new membership statistics book to check the size of parishes served by seminary classmates. Some denominations collected funds from local congregations based on the number of members.

This approach made sense for congregations concerned with meeting the needs of current members. Often membership increases were celebrated as evangelism victories. The power of "immigration evangelism" and "maternity ward evangelism" was unsurpassed. In most cases, formal evangelism programs had little to do with membership gains.

In the unchurched society, the focus is on reaching people who are not already members. Average weekly worship attendance is a better indicator of the life, health, strength, and vitality of congregations. Callahan and others urge counting constituents, people served in mission, and the number of new significant relational groups started as more helpful measures.[2] In fact, these numbers are more than end-of-year benchmarks. Rather, they are central to planning and goal setting for the congregation's future.

In the unchurched society, congregations that seek to reach other people understand that flexibility and variety are important attributes of programming. Unchurched people are not willing to spend years learning to appreciate traditions. Unchurched people will only participate in congregations that touch their lives in ways the unchurched find meaningful.

In the congregation you attend, over the last ten years what has been the annual

* **average weekly worship attendance? Is this number going up or down? Extend the trend ten years into the future. Are you satisfied with the direction?**

* **number of constituents participating? Do you even have a reasonable guess of this number? Are these people in the building but invisible because they are ignored?**

* **number of people served in mission? Compare this with the number of members. How many people within the congregation does it take to assist one person not in the congregation?**

* **number of significant relational groups begun each year?**

Compare this with the number of new members you receive annually.

_____

_____

_____

_____

_____

TRANSITION 13: Congregations create multiple points of entry.

In the churched society, congregations engaged in many programs and
activities of interest to the members. The monthly calendar was full of
activities. These activities were of two types. Some supported the formal
organization. Boards, committees, altar servers, choirs, and a host of
similar groups met monthly or weekly to manage the affairs of the congregation.

Some activities provided social programs for the members. Groups
of men or women met separately for educational, social, and service
activities. The congregation conducted youth programs for any young
people still participating in the congregation. Sometimes it sponsored
Boy Scouts, Girl Scouts, and similar activities for children.

These activities were of, by, and for the members of the congregation. Once in a while a person from outside the congregation would appear. Sometimes the congregation assured itself that outside people were
always welcome. However, it launched few special efforts to encourage
others to participate.

The few programs designed to reach other people tended to be third-
party, social service programs. Food pantries, clothing drives, homeless
shelters, and similar programs involved assisting others in need. These
third-party programs were usually for the "downtrodden of society."
Most such programs involved fleeting contact—if any—between members and the persons receiving the service. Congregations rented their
facilities to outside organizations as part of what they understood to be
outreach efforts.

The only opportunity most people had to come into meaningful contact with people who were not already members was the weekly worship experience. That one entry point used only one form of communication, one style of worship.

Reaching people in the unchurched culture involves multiple points of contact. Some programs are for current members. Most programs actively seek to include people who are not already members. Many programs encourage and make it possible for members to make meaningful contact with nonmembers.

A wide variety of human needs—of members and nonmembers alike—are addressed by congregations through first-person activities, which help establish meaningful contact between individual members and individual nonmembers. We do more than give someone a hot meal. We eat the meal with a nonmember and then spend time sharing experiences.

The most powerful entry point to the congregation is the weekly worship experience. These services generally use a variety of communication methods, that is, various styles of worship.

Examine several of the monthly activity lists from the congregation you attend. Count how many

* **support the formal organization**

* **primarily involve current members**

* **specifically include nonmembers**

_____

_____

_____

_____

_____

TRANSITION 14: Congregations organize around mission, not maintenance.

Congregations in the churched society were organized around the operational needs of the congregation. Large numbers of boards and committees met at least monthly. Large amounts of time were spent being sure the time-tested programs and activities took place year after year. Last year's program served as the plan for next year's program. Congregations developed elaborate systems of checks and balance. It was assumed that only last year's programs would be conducted next year. All other ideas had to be approved by several layers of administrative structure before being put in place.

Every individual, committee, or board had an area of responsibility. No area of responsibility overlapped with any other area of responsibility. When overlap occurred, decisions were made about which group's authority would be supreme. Large amounts of energy were expended to fill all committee slots for multiple-year terms of office.

Many congregations had one or two specific people with veto authority over any decision. Sometimes this individual was a long-term pastor. Sometimes it was a matriarch or patriarch of the congregation who had not held an elected office for several decades. Sometimes this person was the largest financial contributor. This person had clear and unquestioned authority.

Congregations in the unchurched society are organized around mission. Structure is dismantled if it gets in the way of mission. Difficulty recruiting committee members is a signal to disband the committee, complete the work a different way, or discontinue the activity. Many congregations in the unchurched society have abandoned committees elected for multiple-year terms in favor of action teams or task forces composed of any interested volunteers who make short-term commitments.

The governing body of the congregation sees its role as coordinating the ministry of all groups in an effort to reach people who are not yet members. All boards, committees, action teams, and task forces seek ways to work together to accomplish that task.

No single person or small group is permitted to hold the rest of the congregation hostage. People who insist that the congregation adopt their one-and-only way of doing things are clearly informed that the ministry needs of the congregation come first.

Sensitivity is maintained for the wishes of everyone—including long-

*term members. The congregation undertakes activities desired by the
wide variety of people inside and outside the congregation. A place exists
for everyone who is being served by the congregation.*

**How many times in the last ten years has the congregation to which
you belong modified itself in response to changes in the people it
might serve?**

_____

_____

_____

_____

_____

TRANSITION 15: **Congregations view so-called mistakes as opportunities to learn.**

Congregations in the unchurched society spent large amounts of energy
avoiding mistakes. Each unit of the church had at least one person who
functioned as the archivist of failed programs. Every congregation had
one person who was able to remind the group about an unsuccessful activity ten, twenty, or thirty years ago. These valued people were helpful
in seeing that mistakes were not repeated. When a program failed, there
was usually a formal or informal system of chastising the leader of the
failed program. Members and clergy were taught not to cause a failure.

New people who suggested an idea similar to a prior failure were
politely (or impolitely) informed about problems with their new idea.
The risk associated with a new idea was so high that large numbers of
people participated in the approval process before any new activity occurred. If a new idea that finally received approval eventually failed,
more procedures were added to ensure that the system to screen new
ideas did not fail again.

The systems used in the churched society had two common characteristics. First, people did not trust each other. Second, this lack of trust
meant virtually no individuals were empowered to act.

Effective operation in the unchurched society means there is no such thing as a "mistake." There are programs that do not yield desired results. There are activities that do not achieve intended outcomes. However, any program or activity that does not achieve its purpose is celebrated as a learning experience.

The "archivist" serves helpfully to inform others about similar new ideas. New ideas enjoy the support of people who share insights from prior programs that did not achieve desired outcomes.

People who champion ideas that do not work out are recognized for their passion and commitment. People are made to feel part of the whole ministry, even when they feel embarrassed about not achieving desired results.

Congregations focused on reaching people who are not already members do not spend much time on formal structure. This does not mean they are careless or haphazard. In fact, these congregations are even more intentional about results. The difference is they do not woodenly apply results-based standards.

The systems used in the unchurched society have two common characteristics. First, people have very high levels of trust in each other. Second, this high amount of trust means many people are empowered to act.

Does your congregation encourage or prevent new thinking?

_____

_____

_____

_____

_____

TRANSITION 16: Congregations make maximum use of the "priest-hood of all believers."

The pastor was the primary person who approved virtually all matters in the churched society. In traditions where pastors move frequently, a congregation matriarch or patriarch filled the role of decision maker. These individuals determined the nature and function of the congregation. Nothing happened unless they first approved. Very little happened that they did not find personally appealing. The key role of evangelism was assigned to the pastor or an evangelism committee. The members-at-large were not responsible for the congregation's evangelism outcomes.

The congregation's achievement was limited by the time and abilities of a specific key leader. When that leader was the pastor, the congregation often required that the pastor attend most gatherings. Members felt offended if the pastor was not present for *their* meeting or activity. The pastor handled time commitments by keeping the number of activities to a manageable number.

The pastor's time was totally consumed by regular ministry with current members and attending meetings. Members may have expressed dismay that more was not happening in the congregation, but they were not interested in changing the system that allocated the pastor's and other leaders' time in a manner that prevented new activities. This arrangement made the ministry dependent upon the time and abilities of the pastor or other key leaders.

Congregational activity in the unchurched society requires active leadership by a wide variety of people. Congregations that understand this requirement exhibit high levels of trust. Clergy, elected leaders, and members trust each other.

Developing new ways of reaching people is everyone's responsibility. Some congregations, aware of the realities of the unchurched society, do not have evangelism committees. They fear that delegating evangelism to a small group of people undermines the desired goal of the congregation as a whole. If the congregation has an evangelism committee, it is a teaching group, not just a doing group.

The leaders of these congregations work to remind members that the overall mission of the congregation is as an outpost on a mission field. Members actively develop and operate the programs of the congregation.

How many different people have helped a new person come to participate in the congregation you attend? How many different people have "permission" to create a program or activity?

_____

_____

_____

_____

_____

Denominational Transitions

Many church people know about the seven transitions listed in chapter 1 and the nine transitions listed so far in this chapter. The implications of change in our society for regional and national structures are less clear. The next four transitions are outgrowths of the prior sixteen transitions that researchers did not expect to find when they looked at congregations.

Several of these transitions are hard to accept. They contradict widely held views about the role and function of regional and national denominational personnel. They imply roles substantially different from those for which regional and national personnel were hired.

Transitions 17 through 20 suggest substantially more than that denominations modify current practices. For some denominations, these transitions imply that denominations need to reengineer their functions. Members who understand the first sixteen transitions will readily identify with the next four. Many other people will find these difficult to accept.

TRANSITION 17: Congregations are unique.

In the churched culture, congregations tended to be similar to each other. What worked in one congregation would work fairly well in most other congregations.

Characteristics of congregations were stable over long periods of time. The congregational life experienced by one generation was similar to what the next generation experienced. Children and youth enjoyed basically the same activities as their parents and grandparents. Families could count on the same worship experiences and social activities from one generation to the next.

The list of skills needed by clergy did not change from one decade to the next. Abilities effective in one congregation would also be effective in most other congregations. Leadership skills learned by clergy during seminary training were useful for an entire career. Skills learned by seminary faculty during their time in congregations ten, twenty, or thirty years before were still valid for future clergy.

Loss of denominational loyalty coupled with separation of "faith" from "congregational participation" has had a dramatic effect on congregations that seek to reach people who are not already members. Each congregation finds itself on a unique mission field. Each congregation discovers the need to use communication styles appropriate to the community. Each congregation understands the unique capabilities of its leaders, volunteers, and neighbors.

In the unchurched society, Great Commission congregations are different from one to the next. Congregations hold firmly to the unchanging truths confessed by their denomination, but at the same time, congregations develop methods of communicating those truths in ways that are appropriate to their local mission fields.

Specific activities of congregations change to fit the needs of their current environment. Programs effective five years ago might not yield desired results today. Activities appreciated by parents and grandparents are often scorned by their children and grandchildren.

The congregational experiences of those who train clergy are different from what their students are about to encounter. The congregational experiences of long-term regional and national office personnel do not match what congregations are currently experiencing. People who attempt to assist congregations cannot rely on the understanding of congregations they developed ten or twenty years ago in their congregational careers. Keeping up with congregational realities has become a major challenge.

Visit a congregation in which large numbers of adults are converting to or reaffirming the Christian faith (as distinguished from transferring active membership from another congregation). Interview participants in that congregation about their activities. Compare a list of their activities with lists of your congregation's activities twenty years ago and today.

_____

_____

_____

_____

_____

TRANSITION 18: Congregations look beyond denominations, and especially to other congregations, for materials.

In the days of the churched society, what worked for one congregation could generally work for most other congregations. The total number of programs or activities needed in a denomination was relatively small. Congregational characteristics were stable over long periods of time. Relatively few new programs or activities needed to be developed each year.

The denomination was able to function as the sole source of resources for congregations. Virtually no congregations had volunteer leaders with the skills needed to design, develop, and implement programs and activities. Instead, denominations hired staff experts to develop all kinds of materials for use by congregations. The experts wrote worship, evangelism, stewardship, and instructional materials for people of all ages, and denominations established publishing arms to develop printed materials. These publishing units sold their materials almost exclusively to congregations of their own denominations. "Brand loyalty" was strong, so publishers could rely on steady levels of annual sales to the denomination's congregations. Sales outside the denomination were not important to the financial survival of the publisher.

Congregations relied exclusively on denominationally supplied materials, programs, and training. They wanted prepackaged materials developed for the culture, methods, and procedures characteristic of their denomination. They also counted on denominational publishers for doctrinal propriety and procedural integrity. People within congregations did not feel qualified to select program materials, and only the rare congregation would venture beyond its own denominational resources for materials. In some traditions, going outside the denomination for resources was thought to present dangerous exposure to false doctrine.

Most congregations within any given denomination were fairly similar to one another, so programs written by the central source generally worked in most congregations. Regional officials could simply take a program "off the shelf" with confidence that the congregation would benefit from the denominationally designed program. Local people used the program "right out of the box" without modification.

In the unchurched society, each congregation finds itself on a unique mission field, and what works for one may not be effective for another a short distance away. The total number of congregational programs and activities needed in any denomination is staggering. Many congregations find that the mix of resources and needs changes at least once a decade. Remaining effective at reaching unchurched people means staying alert and flexible. Great Commission outreach congregations constantly look for new, effective ways to achieve outreach, and they secure new ideas from almost any available source.

The denomination's materials are not automatically assumed to be the best for the congregation. Congregations no longer assume denominational materials can be taken off the shelf and used directly out of the box in their situations. Denominational publishing units must compete with a broad array of suppliers. Marketing methods now permit even the smallest mom-and-pop publishing shop to market materials worldwide. Pressure on denominational publishing companies is extreme. No longer can denominational publishers rely on substantial annual sales volume to congregations affiliated with their denominations.

Congregations possess many members with expertise in a wide variety of specialties, including planning, programming, training, fund raising, communications, construction, general management, music, group relations, Scripture study, and a host of other disciplines. Congregations are no longer dependent on denominations to select or design materials

*needed in the congregation's unique situation. In fact, they often find
their most effective learning occurs through contact with other congregations. When a particular ministry problem or need surfaces, they look
for another congregation in similar circumstances that has solved the
problem.*

*A growing number of nondenominational conferences offer training
in a wide variety of areas. Many are staged by individual congregations
willing to share what they have learned. Most Great Commission outreach congregations are comfortable going outside their denomination
to learn methodology without fear of compromising their theology.*

**Examine the materials used in your congregation. From how many
different publishers does the congregation purchase resources?
Contact the leaders of a congregation in your area that is experiencing rapid expansion of their mission and ministry. Ask the leaders
where they go for new ideas or for help solving problems.**

TRANSITION **19: Regional denominational offices relate differently to
congregations.**

In the churched culture, it was efficient and effective to centralize in a
regional staff people with program expertise. When major new programs
became available, regional program experts held workshops to teach the
new methods. When a congregation had a specific need, a regional
expert would be contacted. Most regional and denominational meetings
included sessions on how to deal with common problems.

Regional personnel could rely on the programs, activities, and
methods they had personally used in congregations. Having in-depth
knowledge of each congregation was not a requirement for being helpful.

Most regional personnel were hired because of specific expertise in a certain program area. They were responsible for that program area within their region. If a congregation called the regional office with a question, the caller was referred to the appropriate expert. For example, a caller asking "What can we do to involve more youth in our congregation?" would be transferred to the staff person working with youth programs.

Regional offices received sufficient financial support to fund program staff in each of several program areas. Administrative needs of regional program boards and committees were met. Time was still available to be helpful to individual congregations.

Growing awareness of congregational individuality in the unchurched society has generated a need to know the congregation intimately in order to be helpful. Expertise in specific content areas is helpful, but advisors must be experienced in, not just familiar with, individual congregations.

Setting up networks between congregations that are experiencing problems and congregations that have discovered solutions becomes a key regional staff role. Congregations do not call regional offices; they call the staff person who serves as liaison to that congregation.

Calls for help are handled as invitations for a visit. A trusted regional staff person often finds the real problem is different from the one for which help is requested. A church that says it has a problem getting youth to participate might really be a congregation with a leadership issue—young people are not part of youth program planning.

As regions experience declining financial support, they assign fewer staff people to more program areas. Administrative needs of program boards and committees grow. Staff carry larger portfolios of program responsibilities. The ability to help individual congregations is seriously undermined.

For regional staff who respond to Great Commission outreach congregations, some content expertise is still helpful, but it is more helpful to be an effective gateway manager or network developer. Linking congregations with problems to congregations with solutions becomes the most efficient and effective method for regions to work.

How is your denomination's region staffed—by program experts or network managers? How much affinity do the congregations in your region feel toward the regional office?

TRANSITION **20: National denominational offices relate differently to congregations.**

Denominational structures supported many different activities helpful to congregations in the churched society. They administered worker benefit programs, mission programs, educational institutions, public relations efforts, and government relations functions.

In the churched society, most denominations devoted significant amounts of money to support congregational activities. Using the same "centralization of experts" philosophy practiced on the regional level, they assembled staffs of program area experts. These professionals designed and developed programs for congregations. Support for this approach was extensive throughout most denominations. Members of congregations had positive attitudes toward the denomination as a whole, appreciated the leadership provided by denominational program personnel, and were pleased to make financial contributions to denominational efforts.

Congregations' growing sense of individuality creates major changes in the relationship between Great Commission-oriented congregations and their denominations. These congregations find that other congregations are more helpful then the denomination, and they less frequently purchase programs developed by denominational experts.

A feeling of distance between congregations and the denomination has developed. Distancing has lead to congregations reassigning congregational resources that were once passed on to support denominational efforts. Decreasing funding of denominations has resulted in fewer experts producing fewer programs of use to fewer congregations. A downward spiral of cause and effect has resulted in congregations being less effective and denominations having decreasing impact on congregations.

Regional and national staff have become demoralized. They describe their work as "putting out fires." And yet, they seem unable to break old habits and to start focusing on preventing fires.

The challenge for denominations lies in celebrating the variety of congregations in the unchurched society. Many denominational leaders feel threatened by a sense that they are losing control over what is going on in congregations. Successful responses lie in embracing, understanding, and working with the realities of congregations.

Several changes are emerging. Denominations augment their rela-tively few programs with hundreds of good ideas being developed outside the denomination. Denominations support the idea that congregations can find good ideas, resources, and assistance in many places, not just from denominational personnel. Denominations recognize hard copy, electronic, and relational networking as useful tools. Denominations are starting to embrace whatever is helpful to congregations, rather than jealously guarding against intrusion by others.

Name three good ideas, helpful to congregations, that you have seen used by congregations outside your denomination. What would it take for those ideas to be utilized in your denomination?

_____

_____

_____

_____

_____

Transitions Affecting Everyone

The last two transitions are both general and specific, complex and sim-ple. They describe overarching concepts and specific activities providing a general framework for the prior twenty. In one sense, it might have been helpful to provide these at the beginning of chapter 1. In another sense, understanding these last two requires detailed knowledge of the prior chapters.

TRANSITION 21: **Uniformity is being replaced by choices and para-doxes.**

In the churched society, the goal was to design the one best program or activity to meet a challenge. Program experts consumed considerable amounts of time and money designing the best programs for all congregations. Mission experts argued about and then settled on the one, best method to approach a mission opportunity. Fund raisers worked hard to produce the one, most effective way to raise funds.

Publishers produced and then sold materials designed to provide the one, best way to transmit knowledge and beliefs. Planning experts developed the one, best way for congregations to manage themselves. Musicians and liturgists held hundreds of heated discussions about the one or two best ways to conduct weekly worship.

In most traditions, there was one, best way to operate a congregation. That method was taught in seminary. That method was administered by denominational officials. Some traditions were exceptionally autocratic, while others were more subtle in their insistence on using the accepted method. Virtually all denominations ostracized individuals who sought to use different approaches.

Generally, the definition of the one, best way to proceed was based on the personal experience of the final decision maker. But an important factor should never be overlooked. In the churched culture the system worked.

The strengths of the churched society have become the undoing of congregations, regions, and denominations in the unchurched society. In the unchurched society, the goal is to surface hundreds of programs or activities to meet ministry challenges. Thousands of program experts are developing effective programs for all different kinds of congregations. Mission experts understand there are many ways to pursue a mission opportunity. Fund raisers are producing effective fund raising methods targeted at a wide variety of people with different interests.

Publishers are producing and selling different types of materials appropriate to the wide variety of congregations and leaders. Planning experts have developed dozens of effective schemes by which congregations can manage themselves. Musicians and liturgists are compiling thousands of songs and hundreds of effective and theologically correct ways to conduct weekly worship. The watchword is choices.

Make a list of the approaches, programs, procedures, or other activities in your church that you think are not as effective as you would like. Pick the two or three about which you have the most concerns. Find someone within your denomination who uses that activity. Ask

that person to spend thirty minutes helping you understand what they find useful about the activity.

TRANSITION 22: **Control is being replaced with trust.**

Just under the surface within the churched society lay efforts to control. Surveys never asked about it, and some church people disliked being identified with it. Many church people tolerated control only when they were the ones in control. But without a doubt, throughout the churched society, the desire for control, closely related to the expectation that uniformity would prevail, was a key.

In the churched society, liturgists sought to have every congregation use the approved form of worship—control. Program developers attempted to define the best way to conduct the ministry in which they were expert—they exercised control. Denominational officials decided what was best for local congregations—they sought control. Pastors, the matriarch, or the patriarch decided what was best for the congregation—they had control. Volunteer congregation leaders, kicked around by many of their life circumstances, found themselves in a position to make others conform to their views—they demanded control.

Searching for the one best way to do things was viewed, not unreasonably, as good stewardship of time and talent. In the churched society, a control philosophy worked because most people were willing to accept the expert's opinion about the one best method. The relatively few who objected were not missed after they were forced to agree or leave.

In congregations that effectively deal with the unchurched society, it is obvious that clergy and laity trust each other. Denominational and regional people trust congregations, and congregations return that trust.

People trust each other in mission and ministry. They do not always understand each other, but they trust each other. They concentrate on mission and ministry, rather than on administration.

Disagreement is viewed as an opportunity to grow in understanding, not as an opportunity to exert control. People listen to those with different ideas so they can learn, not criticize. The phrase "That doesn't make sense!" is replaced by "I don't understand."

Trust and respect for others does not necessarily produce a free-for-all. It means we agree on the goals, and you decide what methods will work best in your ministry. It means when goals are not met, we all try to help fix the problems.

Think about the church person with whom you have the most serious disagreement. Write out the words you will say when you next encounter that person, starting with, "Help me understand what you mean when you say..."

_____

_____

_____

_____

_____

Dealing with All the Transitions

You probably agree with only some of the twenty-two transitions listed in chapter 1 and this chapter. Five steps, however, will help you at least absorb them:

1. Mark the transitions you think are accurate.
2. Mark the two or three transitions with the strongest impact on your ministry.
3. Choose one of the high-impact transitions and pick a time (write it in

your personal calendar) when you will devote fifty-five minutes to considering it further.

4. Ask another person whom you respect but really do not know very well to join you in that discussion.
5. Repeat steps three and four for the remaining two transitions.

Accurate	High Impact		
_____	_____	1.	We have shifted from a churched society to an unchurched society.
_____	_____	2.	People participate in congregations for different reasons.
_____	_____	3.	People have less loyalty to denominations
_____	_____	4.	Congregations have different purposes.
_____	_____	5.	The mission field has moved.
_____	_____	6.	Different people do the mission work.
_____	_____	7.	Different denominational communication systems are developing.
_____	_____	8.	Congregations focus beyond current membership.
_____	_____	9.	Congregations defend faith by proclaiming the faith.
_____	_____	10.	Unchurched people have faith.
_____	_____	11.	Joining a congregation is a six-step process.
_____	_____	12.	Worship attendance and the number of people served, not membership, tells the story.
_____	_____	13.	Congregations create multiple points of entry.
_____	_____	14.	Congregations organized around mission, not maintenance.
_____	_____	15.	Congregations view so-called mistakes as opportunities to learn.
_____	_____	16.	Congregations make maximum use of the "priesthood of all believers."
_____	_____	17.	Congregations are unique.
_____	_____	18.	Congregations look beyond denominations, and especially to other congregations, for materials.

_____   _____   19. Regional denominational offices relate dif-
                            ferently to congregations.
_____   _____   20. National denominational offices relate dif-
                            ferently to congregations.
_____   _____   21. Uniformity is being replaced by choices and
                            paradoxes.
_____   _____   22. Control is being replaced with trust.

For Reflection and Discussion

If you are reading this book with a group, ask each group member to
follow the approach described for individual consideration of the transitions. Then write the numbers 1 through 22 down the left side of a sheet
of newsprint, a chalkboard, or a white board. Draw a line down the middle of the sheet or board, from top to bottom. Label the left side disagree
and the right side agree. Ask each person to mark whether he or she
agrees or disagrees with each transition (or give each person peel-off
dots to use to vote).

    After seeing how your group feels about each item, pick those tran-
sitions the group would most like to discuss. Use these important guide-
lines for your discussion:

1. Spend a total of ten (not eleven or more) minutes "trashing" *all*
the transitions with which everyone disagrees.

2. Spend thirty to sixty minutes discussing each of the transitions
that most people in your study group think will be helpful to your
ministry.

CHAPTER 11

Great Commission Outreach

A literature search of over 100 titles, eleven formal studies, and four informal studies conducted over two years and costing over $1 million generates a large amount of information. Most research efforts of this size create conflicting opinions. Most investigations of this magnitude and complexity lead in several directions. Such was not the case with the Church Membership Initiative. In fact, an outside researcher would be suspicious that so much work by so many different people using different methodologies could reach the same relatively few simple conclusions. But as people of God, we are aware that it is possible to feel the hand of God leading believers. That seems to have happened in this project.

The few simple conclusions reached by this project are:

1. There are problems in organized religion. Data about membership growth and retention, Great Commission outreach, and other key factors are discouraging for most mainline denominations.

2. The change from a churched society to an unchurched society has had profound effects on organized religion.

3. The changed relationship between church and society and the resulting problems in the church are rooted in sociology, psychology, anthropology, and demographics. Unfortunately, organized religion has not had much success influencing the root sources of church problems. The fact that denominations have concentrated so much energy on the larger society led to Peter Drucker's insightful observation about the church at large, "Their mission became subordinated to social causes. Any organization that forgets its mission dies."

4. We can only deal with the aspects of our problems that are under our control.

5. Congregations are the key. Denominations are no stronger than the collective strength of their individual congregations.

6. A few congregations (perhaps 20 percent) are becoming stronger places of mission and ministry. Most congregations (perhaps 80 percent) are experiencing stable or weakening mission and ministry.

7. Growth and size are not the issue.

8. The primary characteristic that distinguishes growing congregations from stable or declining congregations lies in what they see as their primary ministry.

9. Most congregations (perhaps 80 percent) define themselves in terms of their current members. These congregations achieve virtually no Great Commission outreach. Most of these congregations are slowly dying.

10. Some congregations (perhaps 20 percent) see themselves in mission to people beyond their current membership. While continuing to do excellent ministry with current members, these congregations focus on Great Commission outreach. They are experiencing growth in mission and ministry.

11. How congregations view themselves and their behavior is not affected by top-down management systems. Congregations in this unchurched society are helped one at a time.

12. Solutions lie within individual, motivated congregations taken one at a time.

Attitude toward Great Commission outreach ministry is the key difference between churches that grow and churches that do not. "Magic pills" make no difference if the congregation has not first decided to be serious about reaching the people in its neighborhood. Small groups, planning systems, community census profiles, each-one-reach-one programs, and other evangelism efforts are not effective in congregations closed to realities of the unchurched society. Confining the congregation's mission to current members limits the ministry to a closed group. Only when the parish's mission is open to outsiders will the ministry have opportunity to be a Great Commission outpost.

How do we conduct ministry?

We have been talking about the definition of ministry and how to conduct ministry. Holy Scripture offers some helpful insights on these two topics.

St. Paul writes in 1 Corinthians 9: "When I am with the Jews I seem as one of them so that they will listen to the Gospel and I can win them to Christ. When I am with Gentiles who follow Jewish customs and ceremonics I don't argue, even though I don't agree" (v. 20 TLB). Paul describes his method of communicating in his mission field. He clearly states his practice of blending into the culture he is trying to reach.

St. Paul also says something truly fascinating: "I don't argue even though I don't agree." How does that match with our methods of ministry? Does that sound like your congregation? Does that sound like your denomination? What an amazing statement! "I don't argue even though I don't agree."

The passage continues with another mission-field statement: "When with heathen I agree with them as much as I can" (v. 21 TLB). The first part of this simple sentence ("I agree with them") talks about fitting in with the people. The second part ("as much as I can") does not mean "sell out your beliefs." These two parts highlight the need to distinguish theology from pseudotheology. Paul has good reasons for exposing the Gospel to what some perceive as risk to proper definitions of faith.

He says: "By agreeing, I can win their confidence and help them" (v. 21 TLB). He continues: "Yes, whatever a person is like, I try to find common ground with him so he will let me tell him about Christ and let Christ save him" (v. 22 TLB).

In current times, "winning their confidence" means building relationships. "Whatever a person is like" refers to everyone, even people *not* like us. "Find common ground" means we need to open the side door, the front door, or to find other means of making contact with people. "Tell him about Christ" means we are called to conduct Great Commission outreach.

Paul concludes these thoughts with a summary of his mission on earth. He writes: "I do this to get the Gospel to them and for the blessing I myself receive when I see them come to Christ" (v. 23 TLB). Touching the lives of people is presence outreach. Touching the lives of people "to get the Gospel to them" is Great Commission outreach.

When we conduct ministry that says, "Our form of music and liturgy is so rich and powerful that everyone should learn it to worship with us," we are also saying, "We will withhold the saving message of Jesus from people who do not like our music and do not understand our liturgy." When we fail to welcome people who come to worship services in causal clothes, we are telling them, "God's Word is not something we will share with people who are uncomfortable in more formal clothing." When we conduct activities solely of interest to us, we display to our mission field that we have no interest in helping outsiders find peace in their life through faith in Jesus.

What is ministry?

Remember your first solo drive in the car. Parents know they cannot remind the child of all the lessons and details, so they search for one guiding word, the most important thing to remember. Parents say things like "be careful" or "be safe" or "drive defensively" before the new driver closes the door.

Think about when a child first ventures off on his or her own. Perhaps parents are leaving the child in the college dormitory room. Maybe the family and close friends are seeing the child off at a military induction center. Sometimes the departure is on a wedding day. Parents, relatives, and friends search for that one most important thing to say. They work hard to find the words that will mean the most. Thoughts like "be safe," "work hard but enjoy yourself," or simply "I love you" are spoken.

Jesus did the same thing. He left us with the one, overriding concept that is far more important than all the detailed lessons taught during his time on earth. Matthew records that immediately before ascending to

heaven, Jesus said, "Go ye therefore and teach all nations, baptizing them
in the name of the Father, and the Son and the Holy Ghost" (Matthew
28:19 KJV).

Jesus did not command us to stay inside our sanctuary, teaching
members and a few others who happen to wander in from time to time,
baptizing one or two people every few years. Jesus did not tell us to concentrate on getting our budgets and reports in order. Jesus did not say we
should set up systems so we can control everyone and be sure everything
is always done pretty much the same everywhere. He did not leave us
with the notion that building his church on earth means taking care of
current members and leaving mission work in our neighborhoods to
others.

The parting direction from Jesus was more important than any of the
thousands of other things Jesus could have said before ascending. Jesus
said, "Go ye therefore and teach all nations, baptizing them in the name
of the Father, and the Son and the Holy Spirit."

For Reflection and Discussion

Discuss how well your ministry is responding to our Lord's Great
Commission.

Church Membership Initiative Study Summaries

The Church Membership Initiative (CMI) provided the majority of this book's content. The project included a review of over 100 books and articles, interviews with two experts in this topic, and eleven formal and four informal studies. Findings from these studies were internal to the project and were not published for a broader audience. This appendix summarizes the principal findings.

The information is reprinted with the permission of Aid Association for Lutherans (AAL). This information is part of a report produced for the CMI project begun by AAL in 1991. The CMI project was encouraged and guided by an advisory group representing several Lutheran church bodies.

Research summary of findings reprinted below contains information shared with advisory church bodies in the context of a gift from AAL to Lutherans. While the findings offered some diagnosis of challenges facing these church bodies, the CMI project was not designed to offer prescriptions or remedies. The analyses, interpretations, and conclusions for the eleven research studies are exclusively those of the individual researchers. Further information and copyright permission for using findings from any particular study can be requested from the listed principal investigator.

Formal Research Studies

Study 1: To identify congregations that are growing and not growing

Principal Investigators

Dr. Kenn Inskeep, ELCA Office of Research, 8765 West Higgins Road, Chicago, IL 60631

Dr. Peter Becker, CenSRCH: LCMS, 7400 Augusta Street, River Forest, IL 60305

Dr. John Isch, Dr. Martin Luther College: WELS, College Heights, New Ulm, MN 56073

Purpose

To understand growth, stability, and decline of individual congregations within the denomination and to identify specific congregations to be sampled in other studies. The stability or decline in membership of whole denominations is more complex than the total figures indicated. Study of specific congregations' growth or decline would provide texture to the complex problem.

Sample

11,087 congregations in the Evangelical Lutheran Church in America
6,023 congregations in the Lutheran Church—Missouri Synod
1,221 congregations in the Wisconsin Evangelical Lutheran Synod

Findings

*   The larger a congregation is, the more likely it is to be growing.

*   Congregations in all size ranges are growing, stabilized, and declining.

*   Specific congregations can be matched to census information about neighborhoods.

Study 2: Congregations in rural settings

Principal Investigator

Dr. Eldor Meyer, P.O. Box 315, Girard, KS 66743-0315

Purpose

To assess the differences between growing and stable or declining congregations in rural agribusiness settings. The attempt was to determine
whether the positive characteristics of growing congregations can be
transferred to those that are not growing. "Rural agribusiness" means the
community has less than 5,000 people and the economy is dominated by
agriculture. Excluded were rural communities relatively close to larger
cities.

Sample

Sixty-five congregations in agribusiness counties in Great Plains states.

Findings

*   Fewer than 5 percent of rural congregations have a plan to grow.
    Those that do plan to grow have a pastor who is enthusiastic about
    that vision.

*   Declining trends in the demographics of the rural setting have be-
    come embedded within the attitudes of the congregations. Because
    the community is declining, it is assumed to be acceptable for the
    congregation to decline.

*   The members acknowledge that this self-defeating attitude must
    change, but they show no interest in making the change happen.
    There are high levels of apathy.

*   The self-esteem of the congregations and pastors in these settings is
    low.

*   New pastors have not been prepared to work with rural realities.

Study 3: Methods of determining congregation readiness for growth

Principal Investigator

Dr. Kent Hunter, Church Growth Center, P.O. Box 145, Columbus, IN 46730

Purpose

To develop a questionnaire that will differentiate congregations ready to grow from those not ready to grow. The tool might be useful to growth experimentation studies. It might also be useful in the private practice of judicatory consultants who help individual congregations.

Sample

Three versions were tested in fifty congregations. On-site interviews were conducted in ten congregations and telephone interviews in ten congregations.

Findings

*   Eight general dimensions were found in most of the instruments used by fifteen congregation consultants. These are: spiritual growth, environment, world views, attitude, leadership, program, openness to change, and assimilation.

*   Five characteristics were also present in most of the instruments. These are: high priority for Bible study, high priority for sacrament, high priority for worship, high priority for prayer, low priority for political manipulation.

*   A scale was developed that yields low and high potential for growth after assessing congregational factors and environmental factors.

*   Initial validity testing yielded encouraging results.

Study 4: Attitudes of former Lutherans about congregation

Principal Investigator

Dr. Russell Bredholt, CRA Research Group P.O. Box 3700, Winter Springs, FL 32708

Purpose

To discover why four million people in the United States who call themselves Lutheran have not joined a Lutheran congregation (they are currently unchurched). To understand why former Lutherans joined congregations of another denomination (they are currently churched). To seek differences in the reasons for withdrawal by (1) people who withdrew from the church when they relocated their residence and (2) people who withdrew but who had not relocated.

Sample: Part One

One focus group of ten former Lutherans who are currently churched, and one focus group of ten former Lutherans who are not now churched.

Findings

* Former members (now churched or unchurched) left because they felt the congregation failed them in their time of greatest need (for example, when they were experiencing divorce, personal crisis, loss of job, emotional difficulties, problems with children, and so forth). Former members frequently used the term "judgmental attitude" (meaning being judged negatively) to describe their perceptions of the way they were viewed or treated by the pastor and members.

* Former members who are now members of another denomination retain some levels of hostility concerning the negative experience that caused them to leave a congregation. They felt the congregation did not help them develop a personal relationship with the Lord and did not provide in-depth Bible teaching. They felt the congregation did not emphasize teachings that help them do God's work every day of the week.

* Former members who are not members of any congregation politely answered questions about what might increase their interest in rejoining a congregation. They affirmed the value of Bible study, better preaching, and other commonly suggested preferences. However, their body language and voice tone strongly suggested they were simply politely answering questions. They displayed no motivation to return.

* These former members did not seem inclined to give the church another chance. Some former members who are not now members of other congregations would not consider rejoining unless they had a deep personal experience (problem, pain, and the like) that caused them to seek help. The problems would probably not appear to them to be directly spiritual in nature. Therefore, reconnecting to the congregation would probably come through side-door entry points, rather than worship.

Sample: Part Two

Telephone interviews of 210 people who identify themselves as Lutheran, but who are not on the membership roster of any Lutheran congregation.

Findings

* Fifty-four percent have been inactive for more than ten years.

* Fifty-nine percent had been members of their last congregation for more than ten years prior to leaving.

* Fifty-six percent were between eighteen and thirty-five years of age (average thirty years).

* Half left when they relocated their residence. The other half had not relocated when they left their last congregation.

* Fifty-one percent had visited a congregation at least once since becoming inactive.

* Six percent are currently active in a church or religious group.

* Eighty-nine percent had *not* been contacted by their former congre-

gations and asked to become more active. Yet 42 percent said they would at least consider becoming more active if asked. This was especially the case for "single, divorced, widowed" people and those twenty-four to forty-four years of age.

* Twenty-nine percent indicated that religion plays a "very important" role in their lives today. An additional 43 percent indicate religion plays a "fairly important" role in their lives today. Combining these two groups shows that 72 percent of unchurched former members feel religion plays at least a fairly important role in their lives today.

* Forty-one percent indicate they pray to God daily. An additional 19 percent report they pray to God weekly.

* The three main reasons for leaving the congregation were relocation, disagreement with beliefs, and availability of time.

* A general observation was made that this group of former members appears to be no different from the population at large. Personal time is the great divider. These people left because they have other, "more important" diversions at this time in their lives.

Study 5: What new adult Lutherans experienced when they joined a Lutheran congregation

Principal Investigators

Mrs. Anndel Hodges and Dr. Andy Martin, Opinions Unlimited, Inc., P.O. Box 50515, Amarillo, TX 79159

Purpose

The literature search uncovered large quantities of information about unchurched people's attitudes and feelings about church. Much of this literature suggests things that might be done to encourage unchurched people to affiliate with a congregation. This study compared the experience of people who recently joined a Lutheran congregation with data from studies of the unchurched. The intent was to verify whether the outreach suggestions seem to be effective.

Sample

Telephone interviews were conducted with 280 randomly selected new members from forty growing, thirty-four stable, and twenty-six declining membership congregations.

Findings

*   Sixty percent of new members had transferred from another congregation in the same denomination. Of this transferring 60 percent, one-quarter had been out of a congregation for over two years.

*   Moving was the reason 56 percent of these people left their former congregations. Twenty-eight percent reported problems with the pastor/staff, doctrinal problems, or personal problems as the reason for leaving.

*   Personal contact by a friend, congregation member, or pastor were the most frequently cited reasons for becoming aware of the newly joined congregation. Self-referral ("I wanted a church") was the most often cited reason for the first visit to the congregation.

*   When they visited the new congregation, these new members considered characteristics associated with fellowship (people, pastor, atmosphere, spirit, and feeling comfortable) to be the most important in determining their first impressions.

*   New members rated spiritual insight as the strongest reason for seeking their new congregation. The main reason for joining was that they wanted a church and looked this one up (43 percent).

*   New family reasons, such as recent marriage or child birth, were offered by 20 percent of respondents, and previous family reasons, such as how parents raised them were cited by another 10 percent. Other reasons for joining included Bible study, the congregation's special attempts to meet them, and preference for the type of worship service offered.

* Most of these new members visited the congregation more than ten times before joining.

* Just over half of the new members are active in congregation activities beyond weekly worship or Bible study.

* Most congregations with shrinking membership were not able to provide the name of even one person who joined their congregation in the prior twelve months.

Study 6: Why nonmember parents of children in Lutheran parochial schools and day care programs do or do not join Lutheran congregations

Principal Investigator

Dr. Peter Becker, CenSRCH, 7400 Augusta Street, River Forest, IL 60305-1499

Purpose

Many Lutheran parochial schools (elementary schools and child care centers) have a large enrollment of people who are not members of the congregation. The study sought to discover why these people do not join the affiliated congregation.

Sample

Fourteen focus groups with non-Lutheran parents who sent their children to a Lutheran elementary school or day care facility were held in five locations across the country.

Findings

* Only a few nonmember parents were unchurched.

* These nonmembers sent their children to the school to receive a Lutheran education, a Christian education, a private education, or to avoid inadequate public schools.

* Little distinguished congregation members' from nonmembers' reasons for sending their children to the Lutheran school or child care center.

* Active members of other congregations will not join the school's congregation.

* People are most open to joining the congregation during life change events (relocation, divorce, death, marriage). Typically they do not join because of school participation. Most do not want to be "pushed" into joining the congregation. A two- or three-year "incubation" period including warmth, acceptance, information classes, and openness from the pastor seems to be needed. A rich diversity of programs to serve people in life situations seems to provide the needed entry points.

* Such issues as congregation members' opposition to the school, cliques, perception of divisiveness, and rules regarding parent membership dissuade nonmember parents from joining.

* Many people with children in a congregation's school or child care center are looking for a culturally compatible style in a congregation in which they might participate.

Study 7: Membership experience in new congregations

Principal Investigator

Mrs. Patricia Neal, Market Insights, Suite 302, 9415 W. Forest Home Avenue, Hales Corners, WI 53130

Purpose

Much of the literature describes establishing new congregations as the most effective way to increase membership. Some people suggest new church planting is the most effective way to achieve denominational membership gains. The first part of this study analyzed membership patterns in new congregations. The second part attempted to discover key factors in new congregations that cause them to achieve membership increase.

Sample: Part One

Ten years of data on fifty-four congregations started in 1980.

Findings

*   After ten years of formal operation, the average (median) weekly worship attendance was seventy-nine people.

*   Fifty percent of congregations had virtually the same average weekly worship attendance and number of members as when they opened.

*   Twenty percent of congregations increased membership but had the same average weekly worship attendance as when they opened.

*   Ten percent of congregations increased membership and attendance for five years. However, by the end of ten years average weekly attendance had fallen back to the size when opened.

*   Twenty percent of congregations increased both membership and weekly worship attendance over their first ten years of existence.

Sample: Part Two

Three hundred eighty-seven telephone interviews of randomly selected members of 49 congregations formed in 1980, 1985, and 1990.

Findings

*   Word-of-mouth and other contacts were the primary reasons for visiting a new congregation. Very few visited a congregation because of outreach, visitation programs, or advertising.

*   Forty-one percent visited only one congregation and 36 percent visited two or three before selecting a new church home.

*   Seventy-nine percent transferred from another congregation of the same denomination.

*   Moving was the primary reason for joining another congregation. A second reason was to leave an undesirable situation at the former congregation.

*   A collection of "people" factors is the most important reasons for joining or not joining a congregation. These included friendliness of members (12 percent), friendliness of pastor (12 percent), pastor's personality (11 percent), and welcome feeling (7 percent). People factors represented 42 percent of the most important reasons for joining. Also noted were the congregation's teachings and affiliation of the congregation with a specific church body (17 percent).

*   Visits by the pastor after first attendance at worship, before joining, were reported by two-thirds of people who eventually joined the congregation. This happened more frequently in the congregations formed in 1990 than those formed in 1980.

*   Thirty percent of the people who joined these new congregations did so within one month of their initial visit. An additional 25 percent joined within two months. An average of 9.36 visits were made before originally joining the congregation.

*   These new members want their congregation to grow. Seventy-six percent of these people have invited at least one person in the past twelve months to attend their congregation.

Study 8: Why some congregations do not grow

Principal Investigator

Dr. Roy Oswald, The Alban Institute, Inc., Suite 433N, 4550 Montgomery Avenue, Bethesda, MD 20814

Purpose

This is the first of four studies intended to discover what might be done to motivate congregations that are not motivated to reach people who are not already members.

Sample

Twelve congregations experiencing membership decline even though located in high growth potential communities

Findings

* The majority of the people in these stable/declining congregations described their congregations as warm and caring places. They were not able to see that visitors found this "closeness" to be "closedness" that excludes outsiders. They had no strategy for assimilating visitors or new members into their congregation. They had no strategy for reaching non-Christians.

* The majority of the members of these stable/declining congregations were surprised by feedback that the congregation had strengths. Members of these congregations seemed conditioned to adopt a "poor me" attitude about their congregation. The researchers had the feeling that this positive feedback might be key in building an exciting future for the congregation.

* These stable/declining congregations do not exhibit a sense of purpose or vision. For these congregations, the denomination's name is more a sign of affiliation than a symbol of vision or purpose.

* These stable/declining congregations were concentrating on maintaining their corporate life. They are intent on maintaining their current attitudes and behaviors which are attractive to a shrinking number of people. They seem unwilling to offer experiences that are seen as enriching by either visitors or long-term members who are changing their preferences.

* These stable/declining congregations ignore their past membership decline and then compound their difficulties by declining to change their attitude or behavior. This is shown by the 86 percent who state they expect membership to maintain or grow.

Study 9: Motivations for growth

Principal Investigator

Dr. Russell Bredholt, CRA Research Group, P.O. Box 3700 Winter Springs, FL 32708

Purpose

This is the second of four studies intended to discover what might be done to motivate congregations that are not motivated to reach people who are not already members.

Sample

In-depth interviews were conducted with clergy and lay leaders in six congregations experiencing membership growth and six congregations experiencing membership decline.

Findings

* Vision, mission, guidance, and a realistic understanding of congregation capability seem to be key factors in congregations experiencing increases in membership.

* Environment (that is, location of congregation, employment patterns, population trends, physical condition of property) seem to have a limiting effect on nongrowing congregations. In some circumstances even strong leadership and desire to reach out into the community may not be enough.

* All congregations indicated a willingness to reassess their current way of operating except in matters of doctrine.

* Congregations do not see themselves as being especially effective in their ability to evangelize non-Christians.

* Lay members tend to view their congregation from the perspective of their individual activity within the congregation. They tend not to see the bigger picture of evangelism opportunities outside

the congregation. This limited vision can be a barrier to moving the congregation forward.

* Virtually every congregation is going through generational change. Clergy and lay leaders who either do not recognize what is happening or do not have training to deal with this kind of situation seem to be having the most difficulty with this transition.

* There are some stable/declining membership congregations that appear to be "held hostage" by a small number who oppose change of any kind.

* Stable/declining membership congregations are aging, both in length of time in existence and the age of the members.

Study 10: Effective leadership in growing congregations

Principal Investigator

Dr. Anne Marie Nuechterlein, Wartburg Theological Seminary, 333 Wartburg Place, Dubuque, IA 52003-7797

Purpose

This is the third of four studies intended to discover what might be done to motivate congregations that are not motivated to reach people who are not already members.

Sample

Clergy and between two and ten lay people were interviewed in twenty congregations experiencing increases in membership.

Findings

* Congregations experiencing increases in membership place "caring for people" at the heart of their ministry. For them, ministry is about

relationships with God, parishioners, local people, and people throughout the world.

* Ministry is drawing people into leadership by helping them discover their gifts. This activity involves surfacing people with ministry gifts, empowering people to use their gifts, assimilating of new people, growth, development, and nurture.

* There is a partnership between the clergy and laity. For them, ministry is partnership, not "my" ministry. It is ministry within the parish and beyond. The concept of the "priesthood of all believers" is key.

* These congregations focus on the Word in new ways. They preach, teach, and discuss how the Word gives meaning and hope in the real world. They seek to help people apply God's Word to their lives by providing a supportive atmosphere. They offer variety and options as a means of inviting people to come to Christ and then to go into the world.

* These congregations exhibit a strong spirituality. They see their work as guiding people to live in an awareness of their relationship with God and to incorporate the Word of God in their lives. They take Scripture and prayer seriously. The atmosphere in the church community is supportive of individuals.

* These congregations have a strong vision that is implemented in imaginative and creative ways. Laity are directly involved in forming that vision.

* There is high sense of identity and positive self-esteem. The congregations convert conflict into positive growth. They use a variety of leadership styles. They are not bound by tradition. They are willing to take risks, dream dreams, and imagine what could be done. They communicate effectively and build supportive relationships.

* Congregations that are experiencing membership increases feel passion for their ministry.

Study 11: Apathy Buster Kit

Principal Investigator

Dr. Kent Hunter, Church Growth Center, P.O. Box 145, Columbus, IN 46730

Purpose

This is the fourth of four studies intended to discover what might be done to motivate congregations that are not motivated to reach people who are not already members.

Sample

The "kit" was field tested in seven congregations.

Findings

* The field test showed that much of the success of the program depends upon the initiative, effort, motivation, and skills of the leadership—key lay leaders and pastor

* Additional field testing of the kit is needed.

Informal Research

Principal Investigator: All four studies

Dr. Alan Klaas, Change Mentoring Partnership, P.O. Box 2844, Appleton, WI 54913

Clergy interviews

Purpose

Gather clergy opinions about the reasons congregations experience membership growth or decline.

Sample

Sixty-two parish pastors in nine locations from a cross section of congregation settings and growth experience were interviewed.

Findings

* The most frequent opinion given for membership decreases was the clining "value of church to people." The clergy explained that depeople "do not have time" for church, moved and do not feel inclined to join a new congregation, and simply "got out of the habit" of participating.

* Clergy in congregations experiencing growth in ministry and membership identified worship style and liturgy as a second major cause of declining membership. These clergy suggested that major differences exist among congregation members who highly value traditional worship or liturgy styles and those members, former members, and unchurched people who are not attracted to traditional worship and liturgy styles.

* Many other reasons were given to explain membership decrease. However, they were cited considerably less frequently than the previous two. The main other reasons were: (1) congregations do not want to increase their membership size; (2) seminary training is

inadequate for serving in a parish; (3) congregations do not use a member transfer referral system to receive new members; and (4) congregations do not have an outreach orientation.

* Even if a good member transfer referral system were put into place, most congregations do not seem prepared (either in attitudes or procedures) to respond to church members moving into their area.

Reactions of regional leaders

Purpose

Collect reactions to findings by using questionnaires in a large meeting of the elected judicatory leaders of the Evangelical Lutheran Church in America and the Lutheran Church—Missouri Synod.

Sample

Seventy-five elected judicatory leaders of the Evangelical Lutheran Church in America and the Lutheran Church—Missouri Synod.

Findings

* Lack of evangelism outreach, lack of concern for the lost, and loss of congregation initiative were given as the primary reasons for mem bership decline.

* Being bound by traditions, the decreasing importance of religion to people, and lower levels of loyalty to denominations were identified as contributing to the decline. Lower birth rates and increased mo- bility were also mentioned as important.

* Also cited was that congregations are not keeping up with cultural changes. They are not meeting the needs of people who confront contemporary issues at home, in society, and in the work place.

* These judicatory leaders cited worship style and liturgy much less frequently than parish pastors.

"Mystery shopping visits" to congregations

Purpose

Verify research findings using different people and different methods of simulating nonmembers visiting a congregation.

Sample

Approximately 100 congregations were visited by a variety of study personnel and other qualified people.

Findings

*   After five minutes in the outer hall before services and the first five minutes of the service, the basic mission of the congregation is very clear. After that small amount of time, it is possible to predict the content of most congregation leadership meetings.

*   Most congregations are made up of people who are very warm and friendly to the other members. Except for an occasional handshake by a greeter, visitors are ignored.

*   Congregations that focus on mission beyond current members have a completely different feel from congregations that focus on their current members.

A meeting of sixty-one growing congregations

Purpose

Receive explanations of their experiences from growing congregations. Receive reactions to commonly available tools that claim to help congregations reach more people.

Sample

Three or four people from each of sixty-one growing congregations of various sizes and types of ministry situation.

Findings

* Congregations linked their growth in ministry to discovering specific responses to their ministry opportunity. These discoveries were unique to each congregation within its specific setting. Interviewed people described changes in basic perceptions that resulted in changing some historical practices while preserving the core theology.

* They described "igniter events" that sparked a desire to be in ministry beyond their current membership. Some of these igniter events were positive experiences like the arrival of a key staff person, a building program, installation of a new sound system, or attendance at a particularly stimulating event. Some of these igniter events were negative experiences like rapidly declining membership, financial problems, or difficulties with a called or contract staff person.

* Congregations in communities where English is a second language expressed the need for culture-specific materials and personnel. They also tended to find solutions for themselves, rather than to wait for others to provide assistance.

* Congregations in African-American communities expressed similar concerns about the cultural orientation of resources and a shortage of culture-specific people to staff their ministries. They made suggestions about the value of cultures learning from each other.

* Congregations expressed a strong preference for networking and other opportunities to share their stories with each other. They were particularly appreciative of direct contact with other active and growing congregations.

NOTES

Chapter 2

1. Dean R. Hoge and David A. Roozen, *Understanding Church Growth and Decline* 1950-1978 (New York: Pilgrim Press, 1979).

2. Dean Hoge, Benton Johnson, and David Luidens, "What Happened to the Youth Who Grew Up in Our Churches?" *Congregations* (September-October 1992): 3-6.

3. Carl F. Reuss, *Profiles of Lutherans in the USA* (Minneapolis: Augsburg Publishing House, 1982), 47.

4. The Center for Social and Religious Research, "A National Study of Marginal Members," Hartford Seminary, October 1993.

Chapter 4

1. Peter Drucker, "The New Models." Address at the 1991 Church in the 21st Century Conference, sponsored by the Leadership Network, Dallas.

Chapter 5

1. Arlin Rothauge, *Sizing Up a Congregation for New Member Ministry* (New York: The Episcopal Church Center, n.d.).

2. Charles Mueller Sr., "Just Watching...," *Wheat Ridge Ministries* 8 (April 1995): 5.

3. Kennon Callahan, *Twelve Keys to an Effective Church* (New York: HarperSanFrancisco, 1983).

Chapter 11

1. George G. Hunter III, *How to Reach Secular People* (Nashville: Abingdon Press, 1992).

2. Kennon L. Callahan, *Twelve Keys to an Effective Church* (New York: HarperSanFrancisco, 1983).

The Alban Institute:
an invitation to membership

The Alban Institute, begun in 1974, believes that the congregation is essential to the task of equipping the people of God to minister in the church and the world. A multi-denominational membership organization, the Institute provides on-site training, educational programs, consulting, research, and publishing for hundreds of churches across the country.

The Alban Institute invites you to be a member of this partnership of laity, clergy, and executives–a partnership that brings together people who are raising important questions about congregational life and people who are trying new solutions, making new discoveries, finding a new way of getting clear about the task of ministry. The Institute exists to provide you with the kinds of information and resources you need to support your ministries.

Join us now and enjoy these benefits:

CONGREGATIONS: The Alban Journal, a highly respected journal published six times a year, to keep you up to date on current issues and trends.

Inside Information, Alban's quarterly newsletter, keeps you informed about research and other happenings around Alban. Available to members only.

Publications Discounts:

- ☐ 15% for Individual, Retired Clergy, and Seminarian Members
- ☐ 25% for Congregational Members
- ☐ 40% for Judicatory and Seminary Executive Members

Discounts on Training and Education Events

Write our Membership Department at the address below or call us at 1-800-486-1318 or 301-718-4407 for more information about how to join The Alban Institute's growing membership, particularly about Congregational Membership in which 12 designated persons receive all benefits of membership.

The Alban Institute, Inc.
Suite 433 North
4550 Montgomery Avenue
Bethesda, MD 20814-3341